INTRODUCING JOHN PAUL II

Born near Manchester in 1930, Peter Hebblethwaite joined the Jesuits at the age of seventeen. He studied philosophy in France, Medieval and Modern Languages at Oxford, and theology at Heythrop College when it was still in the country.

In 1965 he went to Rome to report on the final session of the Second Vatican Council. As editor of the Jesuit periodical, *The Month*, he was involved in reporting the major ecclesiastical events of the following decade. He travelled widely, and had a special interest in Poland. In January 1974 he received permission to resign from the Jesuits, and remains on friendly terms with them. From 1976 to 1979 he was lecturer in French at Wadham College, Oxford. Then he went to Rome as 'Vatican affairs writer' for *The National Catholic Reporter* of Kansas City.

His many books include *The Runaway Church, The Year of Three Popes*, and *The New Inquisition?* He has also translated Pierre de Calan's *Cosmas, or the Love of God*. He is married, with three children.

Books by Peter Hebblethwaite
available from Collins

THE RUNAWAY CHURCH

Books by Karol Wojtyla
available in Fount Paperbacks

SOURCES OF RENEWAL
LOVE AND RESPONSIBILITY

Peter Hebblethwaite

INTRODUCING
JOHN PAUL II
THE POPULIST POPE

'Second papal election. It matters more,
I suppose, than any other, anywhere.
But perhaps this is only
Christian parochialism.'

(Philip Toynbee, *Part of a Journey*,
An Autobiographical Journal 1977–1979,
Collins, 1981, p. 267)

Collins
FOUNT PAPERBACKS

First published in 1982 by Fount Paperbacks, London

© 1982 Peter Hebblethwaite

Made and printed in Great Britain by
William Collins Sons & Co. Ltd, Glasgow

To Halina Bortnowska

Contents

Preface

Pope John Paul II, as anyone except Rip van Winkle knows, is due to visit England, Scotland and Wales towards the end of May 1982.

Many books have been written about him already. Having previously tried other approaches to John Paul – a biography, a chronicle of one year of the pontificate – it seemed to make sense to provide a guide to his characteristic way of thinking.

Who, in short, is coming to see us? What does he think about the questions that interest British Christians? Are the difficulties we sometimes have in understanding him deeply theological or simply cultural? What does he know about us? How Polish is he, and what does that mean? They are the questions everyone wants to know the answer to before the guest arrives.

The title, *Introducing John Paul II*, was suggested by a minor event that took place on 5 February 1981. A photograph records it, here shown on the back cover of this book. There was an audience for the Foreign Press Club of Rome. I was wearing the *Solidarnosc* badge given to me by Halina Bortnowska, a mutual friend who has helped the Pope with the publication of his books.

Seeing the badge, he assumed that I was Polish and, grasping my hand, introduced himself as 'Jan Paweł, Papież' ('John Paul, Pope'). Having explained that I was not Polish, how I came by the badge, and that we had met twice before in the plane to and from Africa, we talked about Halina. So *Jan Paweł, Papież* having introduced himself to me, it seemed only fitting that I should try to introduce him to others.

But history does not stand still. On Monday, 14 December 1981, the day after martial law was introduced in Poland, Halina appeared on a special *Panorama* programme shot the previous week. In it she said: 'To retreat now would be a disaster. It would deprive us of all hope. If we are to be stopped, it will have to be a crash – a bulldozer meeting a wall. We cannot be stopped in any other way.' After that, it seems unlikely that she would have escaped arrest along with the leaders of *Solidarnosc* at the Lenin Steel Works in Nowa Huta, whom she advised. So this book is dedicated to Halina Bortnowska, wherever she is. She has taught me more about Poland than anyone else – and she goes on with her Polish lesson still, through the dark night of the Polish soul.

It remains to add a note about quotations. Most of those from John Paul since he became Pope come from the precious Bulletins of the Vatican Press Office. They usually anticipate the *L'Osservatore Romano* text of the same day and date. Italics, except where otherwise stated, come from the original text. John Paul uses them a lot. He is a pedagogue. They are the typographical equivalent of a *crescendo*. Translations, again except where stated, are my own. Official documents (encyclical letters, apostolic exhortations, etc.) come in many versions. They are here referred to by their section numbers.

I would like to thank Thomas C. Fox, Editor of *The National Catholic Reporter*, Kansas City, for continuing to encourage me in this strangely neglected field of study.

Oxford
6 January 1982

1

Talk of the Pope

It is not easy to find the right tone of voice to talk about popes. I mean, of course, living popes. Long dead popes are another matter: Catholic or Protestant or Marxist historians can treat the papacy the way they would any other venerable institution, without anyone crying scandal. You can say what you like about the Borgias (especially after seeing the stagey villains who peopled the television series), or the far more ghastly tenth-century popes, few of whom died safely in their beds. No one will charge you with *lèse-papauté*. The convenient distinction between the man and his office permits this freedom: a bad pope is still pope. It can even become a kind of boast or apologetic argument: an institution that can survive such office-holders – just over forty popes are reputed to have bought their way to the top – can survive anything. Its claims to divine foundation are enhanced.

It becomes difficult to talk about popes only as you reach this century. Pius X was canonized by his successor Pius XII in 1954. Does that mean that we are forbidden to point out that the hounding he permitted of so-called 'Modernists' was deeply unjust, unChristian, and had disastrous effects on Catholic intellectual life for the next thirty years? Some would deny this freedom.

Another cause of difficulty in talking sensibly about recent popes is that they tend to be wildly over-estimated in their lifetime. In 1937, for example, René Fontenelle, a French *monsignore* working in the Vatican Secretariat of State, the equivalent of the Foreign Office, wrote: 'This is a pontificate destined to dominate the entire century' (*Sa Sainteté Pie XI*,

Spes, Paris, 1937, p. 15). By the end of the book the author is so persuaded of this thesis that he is able roundly to declare that 'the twentieth century will be known as the century of Pius XI' (ibid., p. 240). The sober historical judgement is that Pius XI was autocratic, unpredictable, choleric and slow to perceive the evils of Fascism and Nazism. No one was saying that publicly in 1937, although Ludwig von Pastor, historian of the papacy and at that date Austrian Ambassador to the Holy See, did confide in a memo: 'He almost always went against the advice given him' (Quoted in *Eastern Politics of the Vatican, 1917–1979*, Hansjakob Stehle, Ohio University Press, Athens, Ohio, 1981, p. 67). What von Pastor was privately calling unpredictability, Pius's apologists endeavoured to present as 'spontaneity'. Fontenelle, for example, relates how, at the opening of the new college of Propaganda Fidei in the early 1930s, the Cardinal Secretary of State, Eugenio Pacelli, was already vesting for Mass when suddenly the Pope burst into the sacristy and supplanted him. This incident was supposed to illustrate his great love for the missions (or 'foreign missions' as they were known at the time) – he simply could not stay away on so important an occasion. But this upstaging of his Secretary of State also shows his rudeness towards subordinates.

It is now possible to write honestly about Pius XI. But writing about a contemporary pope remains just as difficult as Fontenelle found it in the 1930s. And for the same reasons. One cannot bring to the task the detachment of the historian, partly because all the documents are not yet available, but more profoundly because no Catholic Christian can treat a living pope with complete neutrality. He is bound to believe that the pope, any pope, has an important ministry in the Church, and he will rejoice or feel regret in so far as the pope is seen to be fulfilling that ministry or not.

But there are different ways of defining the papal ministry, or the Petrine ministry (as theologians prefer to call it). The papacy is rather like the kind of inkblob used in psychological tests: you can read it according to your own concerns. Some might feel that the service of unity means cracking together the skulls of errant theologians who are alleged to be creating confusion. Others hope that the pope will renounce some of his claims and so be capable of being 'a pope for all Christians'. Some want the pope to be very 'visible' in the Church; others would prefer him to keep a low profile and intervene only when necessary. A complicated pattern of hopes and expectations is at work here.

Some writers seem blithely unaware that there is any problem at all. Claudio Sorgi, for example, writes a regular column in the Sunday edition of *L'Osservatore Romano*, the Vatican newspaper. When John Paul had returned from his round-the-world trip to the Philippines, Japan and Alaska – a little matter of twenty-five thousand miles – Sorgi shared with his readers some thoughts about how well the Pope had stood up to the gruelling experience:

And the Pope? He everywhere welcomed the displays of popular enthusiasm with a great spirit of faith, realizing that all the honour and glory passes through him to reach the Master whose Vicar he is. And yet the Pope contributed most importantly with his personal gifts, his faith and his prayer to ensure that the journey became an important stage in the forward march of the Church in the world.

We all wondered how the Pope managed to be less tired than we were. Perhaps the secret was in his heart and in his continual contact with the Divine Master. I saw the Pope praying in the most demanding moments: perhaps while people were applauding him or while someone was delivering an official address of welcome. From close at hand one could see that the Pope had shut his eyes and that his lips were moving imperceptibly: he was praying.

And when the day was done and the rest of us could think only of going to bed, the Pope shut himself away in

the chapel for a long time, on his knees. If anyone wants to know the secret of the success of this pontificate, I would say that it is enough to watch how and how much the Pope prays. He is in continual contact with God. He cannot fail.
(*L'Osservatore della Domenica*, 1 March 1981)

This is exactly the tone used by *Pravda* in speaking of President Leonid Brezhnev. It is simply court flattery. If written of a dead pope, with a view to his canonization, it would be regarded as extravagant. Applied to a living pope, it is highly dangerous because it discredits the truth it contains. I do not doubt for a moment that Pope John Paul is a man of prayer – though I think he should listen when people make speeches of welcome to him – but it is characteristic of prayer that it escapes the onlooker and cannot be observed. That is why, as Orson Welles said, there are two things you cannot convincingly film: prayer and sexual intercourse. The presence of an observer modifies the act. Nor can a 'praying pope' guarantee the 'success of the pontificate', whatever that means.

Sorgi is a Vatican professional. My second text is an amateur account of a papal audience which appeared in the magazine of the *Travailleuses Missionnaires de l'Immaculée*, a quasi 'secular institute' which is French in origin but has many third world members. The originality of the *Travailleuses* is that their apostolate consists in running first-class restaurants. Their Rome restaurant, Eau-Vive, is internationally famous. It is patronized by cardinals and communists. Now on 25 July 1979 the sisters arrived in St Peter's Square an hour early and so got a place in the front row for the papal audience. The anonymous writer sets the scene:

Our hearts were filled with joy: a joy that showed the hope of those who await the coming of the Lord . . . The Pope, 'sweet Christ on earth', as St Catherine of Siena loved to define him, could not pass by without seeing us. The scene in St Peter's Square, crammed with people, made me think of the multitudes who crowded the streets of Jerusalem to see Jesus pass by. The heat was exhausting, but on everyone's face could be read joy, impatience, enthusiasm. 'Ah! If only we could touch the hem of his garment!'

All this was merely build-up. At long last the Pope arrived:

He ignored a *monsignore* who was trying to prevent him getting close to the crowds. Like Jesus, he gave himself completely, answering all those who stretched out their hands to greet him.

But unfortunately he passed them by. He had not noticed them. Tragedy. Yet in greeting the various groups after his address he mentioned them by name. He had been tipped off after all. They leapt up and down in their Caribbean, African and Asian costumes. Delirium and joy. Finally he approached them and said, though he was barely audible above their cries: 'Know that you have prepared a pope at Eau-Vive.' He meant that he had been to dinner there.

Now this kind of lump-in-the-throat narrative is very common in writing about John Paul. It manages to stay just this side of blasphemy ('If only we could touch the hem of his garment'). And one can quite understand why an Ian Paisley or an Enoch Powell should find it cloying and theologically objectionable. So do many Roman Catholics.

But it is not just writers in *L'Osservatore Romano* or pope-struck sisters who write in this way. A reviewer in *The Tablet* commented on Karol Wojtyla's 1960 book, *Love and Responsibility*:

Even in translation one is aware of a fierce and colossal intellect probing and penetrating the material before it. No issue is avoided, no difficulty is side-stepped and no problem is dodged or glossed over. (David Forrester in *The Tablet*, 24 October 1981, p. 1047)

Quite apart from the question of whether these statements are true or false (and the 'fierce and colossal intellect' is not very illuminating), it is perfectly evident that this work would not have been translated into English at all, had not its author become pope.

The papal office casts its light backwards as well as forwards, covering with its glow minor works and deservedly obscure ancient articles. In some of the biographers, this becomes the theme: 'We-always-knew-he-was-going-to-become-pope'. Here is George Blazynski describing what happened – or perhaps what ought to have happened – on the occasion of Fr Wojtyla's consecration as Bishop, 28 September 1958:

> It was a very dark, dull day, overcast and wet. Inside the cathedral it was almost completely dark, save for the flickering candles. With great ceremony Archbishop Baziak placed the bishop's mitre on Wojtyla's head. Suddenly bright rays of sunshine burst through the stained-glass windows and bathed the new bishop and his mitre in clear, warm light. It was a scene worthy of great religious painters. An eye-witness remembers saying to her brother: 'He'll become Pope one day.' (*John Paul II, A Man from Kraków*, Weidenfeld and Nicolson, London, 1979, p. 69)

Unfortunately she omitted to tell anyone else.

It is time to broaden this discussion. These passages all illustrate the perils of writing about a living pope. The tacit assumption of all of them is that the pope is 'top of the class' in all he does. He is top in prayer, top in philosophy, and he has been, as well, playwright, poet, worker, skier, canoeist, sportsman, etc. Follow that if you can.

But it does not follow from any version of the papal primacy doctrine that the personal talents of the pope need be consummate. Of course one will rejoice when they are, but that is an unexpected bonus. If the papal office is considered in its essential function, that of symbolizing the visible unity of the Church (and perhaps eventually of all Christians), what is required of a pope is not that he should excel in everything but quite simply that he should be able to listen. This was the lesson of the pontificate of Pope John XXIII. He did not seek to impose his own ideas. He was rather an enabler who released activity in others.

Another distressing feature of all the passages quoted on John Paul II should be noted. No one, for all their evident emotional involvement, appears to be paying the slightest attention to what he is saying. Or if they do, they don't let on. It is all form and no substance. The presence is all. It is as though the Pope were supposed magically to be able to change situations simply by appearing – an illusion that was dispelled at Drogheda where his appeal, 'on his knees', for peace, was brutally rejected by the IRA within twenty-four hours.

During the visit to the United States, one of his suite admitted that 'they liked the singer but not his song'. He then added that it didn't matter. At this point the danger of demagogy is added to the myth of the pope as superman. This is where the hagiography, the sycophancy, the lump-in-the-throat prose, the creation of legends, finally end. The truth of the matter is that it is very difficult to see the pope – this pope or any other – straight and plain because so many hopes are invested in him, and so many simply project on to him their own aspirations. No one could fulfil them all.

One of the most curious features of talk about John Paul II is that a myth devised for John XXIII has been applied to him most inappropriately. It is the myth of 'the-good-guy-caught-by-the-bad-guys' of the Roman Curia. It is always plausible, since it is always more convenient and satisfying to blame the 'faceless men' of the Curia than the Pope himself. Here is a classic instance from Fr Francis Xavier Murphy, CSSR, a veteran Vaticanologist who always denies that he is 'Xavier Rynne', author of four books on the Second Vatican Council. He is describing *Redemptor Hominis*, John

Paul's first encyclical – and one should note that a *first* encyclical nearly always tends to offer a 'programme' for the pontificate:

> Replete with extravagant terminology and idiosyncratic doctrinal turns, the 18,000-word document gushed forth in vigorous waves of language that gave the Vatican Congregation for the Doctrine of Faith fits, as its scriveners endeavoured to pull it into shape and cope with its theological content. (*The Papacy Today*, Weidenfeld and Nicolson, London, 1981, pp. 194–5)

This fascinating passage tells us nothing, but it communicates a strong emotion. The key terms are 'gushed forth' (like a force of nature or energumen) and 'scriveners' which tells you exactly what to think about these pettifogging, second-rate, unimaginative plodders who strive – in vain – to edit our hero into banality. In fact there is no evidence at all that John Paul submitted *Redemptor Hominis* to the Congregation for the Doctrine of Faith, the body responsible for preserving orthodoxy.

We are now coming even closer to the heart of the matter. The difficulty in writing about John Paul II is that one's judgements are scrutinized for evidence of loyalty or supposed disloyalty. Thus if one points out the evident fact that John Paul's experience of ecumenism, before his election, was somewhat limited, this is regarded as a major gaffe. Doors close. Yet it is the plain truth. Nor does it follow that John Paul is incapable of learning about other Churches such as the Anglican Communion. Usually people learn through the experience of dialogue which, most unfortunately, is something John Paul cannot fit into his busy schedule. Again, John Paul has been reproached with his ignorance of religious life. The special pioneering, frontier-style of certain religious orders, such as the Jesuits, is beyond his comprehension. The proof is that he found it necessary to impose on the Jesuits 'a personal delegate' answerable only to him. There were grave doubts about the constitutionality of this move.

But now the question arises: who is to point these things out? Or, in traditional theological terms, who is to undertake the task of 'fraternal correction'? There seem to be four main candidates for this perilous role: theologians, writers on the Vatican, Poles and cardinals. Let us look at each group in turn.

Theologians are unlikely to volunteer. They have been intimidated, having seen what happened to Hans Küng and Edward Schillebeeckx. They know that the strictest subordination to the *magisterium* is required of them. So they write wry little articles pointing out that in the Middle Ages the term *magisterium* referred to theologians and not to bishops

The three hundred or so journalists accredited to the Vatican are unlikely to make a move. They have no ecclesial status. They do not wish to be branded as 'self-appointed' critics. They have to think about their jobs, their future, their children. They will not rock the boat.

It might be theoretically possible for some of John Paul's Polish friends to speak frankly to him. But in practice it is not. First because Poles are still pinching themselves in astonishment to make sure that they really do have a Polish pope and that it is not all a dream. He is 'their' pope. The second reason why Poles cannot exercise 'fraternal correction' is that the Polish situation is so grave and perilous that it overshadows all other considerations. And Poles rightly think it would be tragic if we failed to recognize what John Paul can give to all of us.

Perhaps, then, members of the college of cardinals, bound to the Pope by a special bond, also enjoy a special freedom. Some of them claim this special freedom, either on the grounds that they were created cardinals in a previous pontificate or because they voted for the present pope at the conclave. But we know of only one cardinal who has spoken critically to the Pope. He is Cardinal Michele Pellegrino, former Archbishop of Turin, now in retirement. In April 1981 he gave an uninhibited interview in which he raised three points: the atmosphere of fear in the Roman Curia; the need to ordain married men in certain parts of the Church; and the lack of compassion towards priests who wish to resign from the ministry without leaving the Church. Here is a sample:

> We proceed under the banner of fear – or rather we don't proceed at all, because of our fear. I think it betrays a lack of faith, but there could be another reason as well. The eyes of those who hold the greatest responsibility in the Church are not sufficiently open to what is going on in the world. They live in an isolated world surrounded by a few people, and do not keep their finger on the pulse of what the majority are thinking . . .
>
> [On the ordination of married men.] Faced with the dilemma: either maintain at all costs the law of celibacy in its present form, and thus abandon any chance of full evangelization, or opt for the full evangelization which requires the Eucharist and would need a modification of Church law – I believe we must take the second path.
>
> [On priests resigning.] I ask the author of *Dives in Misericordia*, John Paul's second encyclical, to show mercy towards these brothers in Christ. I can think of so many who, if the new regulations are enforced in their full rigour, will turn against the Church when in fact they want to work strongly and effectively with the Church. I find here a lack of sensitivity to 'the signs of the times'. (*Il Regno*, Bologna, 15 April 1981)

But Cardinal Pellegrino's remarks were very much an exception, though many privately share his views.

Cardinal Pellegrino is commonly considered a 'progressive' (whatever the term means). No one ever accused Cardinal Carlo Confalonieri, who was eighty-eight last birthday, of that. But he was rather naughty in an interview he gave to *Il Messaggero*, the Rome daily. 'We Italians,' he declared, 'have a universal vision.' As for the foreigner at present in the Vatican, 'He is out of his element, he needs to study the milieu, and he should seek advice through the properly constituted channels.' Asked for a more direct judgement on John Paul, Confalonieri said: 'I think the last three years have been a time of study for him.' But this judgement merely reflects the disappointment of the Roman Curia at being increasingly bypassed and therefore rendered irrelevant. It is unlikely to make any impression on the Pope.

Faced, then, with such a bewildering diversity of judgement and opinion, how is it possible to say anything reasonably objective about Pope John Paul II? The first answer is to try to master the literary output of the pontificate so far. It has been truly prodigious in quantity. It is difficult to keep one's head in the torrent of words. There are further problems because John Paul uses a closely-knit team of, mostly Polish, speech writers, presided over by Archbishop Giovanni Coppa, to help him compose his literary works. But I am going to suppose that if John Paul is prepared to read out a speech, even if he only saw it five minutes before, then he accepts what it says. So the first way to get to know him is to read him. *Tolle, lege.*

Then a second and complementary principle of interpretation enters in: long before Karol Wojtyla became Pope on 16 October 1978, he already had strong opinions and convictions on what was going wrong in the Church. What he thought was no mystery. He had written and spoken a great deal on such matters. So becoming Pope enabled him to project these opinions and convictions on to a wider screen, a vaster stage. Of course there is always the possibility of change, of 'learning on the job'. But as a general rule, it is the past that will illumine the present and the future. And John Paul's 'past' takes us to Poland.

2

Poland and the Apocalypse

In her novel, *Nuns and Soldiers*, Iris Murdoch says of a Polish character always known as 'the Count' – though he is now a British civil servant: 'Like his father he had, in his own way, interiorized Poland, he was his own Poland, suffering alone' (Chatto and Windus, London, 1980, pp. 13–14). This draws attention to the peculiar intensity of Polish national consciousness. Italians are more relaxed or critical about their national tradition, which is anyway less important than regional sentiment. Germans have been obliged to repudiate a good part of their tradition. But Poles are Poles through and through. They carry their Polishness round with them as though it were a burden strapped to their backs. It would certainly be true to say of Pope John Paul II that he has, in his own way, 'interiorized Poland'.

Apart from two years of study in Rome, 1946–8, he spent his first fifty-eight years in Poland. Even when, as Bishop and Cardinal, he began to travel, his first call was always on Polish communities in exile. Despite his mastery of an astonishing number of languages – and his cheerful readiness to try new and difficult ones such as Japanese or, we may be sure, Welsh – he remains resolutely and defiantly Polish. So far, so obvious.

The difficulty lies in stating how this Polishness affects the pontificate. The temptation is to equate Polishness with conservatism in Church matters. But being Polish is not just a blinkered limitation; it can sometimes provide a different perspective on the world from which we can all learn something – even if it is only that there are other perspectives.

Here is one simple example. Pope John Paul, like his immediate predecessors, regularly uses his Angelus appearances at noon on Sunday as an opportunity to comment on various events or anniversaries. On Sunday, 28 September 1980, many topics must have jostled for the Pope's attention. He dealt briefly with the Synod on the family, which he had officially opened two days before; he noted that later that afternoon he would be going to Subiaco to lead the European Bishops in pilgrimage to 'the cradle of Benedictine monasticism'; and it was the second anniversary of the death of his predecessor, John Paul I, who has gone down in history as 'the smiling pope'. All this was utterly predictable. There would have been complaints had he omitted any of these topics.

But he added a fourth theme and gave it equal treatment:

On this occasion I cannot fail to mention the fact that 30 September will be the hundredth anniversary of the day on which Pope Leo XIII published his encyclical *Grande Munus* which extended the liturgical cult of Saints Cyril and Methodius to the universal Church.

Saints Cyril and Methodius, who came from Thessalonika and belonged to the tradition of Constantinople, worked among the peoples of the Balkans and the Danube basin and were *true apostles of the Slav peoples*. Translating the liturgy into Old Slavonic, they not only made a great contribution to *evangelization* but also to the culture of the Slav peoples, and indeed provided its foundations. (28 September 1980)

It is fair to say that a non-Slav Pope would have been unlikely to have remembered the hundredth anniversary of *Grande Munus*, which is not one of the best-known of Leo XIII's encyclicals. But Poles have a passion for anniversaries, which provide a way of constantly reinterpreting and repossessing their past.

Even more important, however, was the fact that on the

very day when the Euro-Bishops were off to Subiaco to commemorate St Benedict, the patron of Europe, Pope John Paul served notice that he had in view a 'wider Europe', one that was evangelized not just by Benedictine monks coming from Rome or the West, but by monks in the tradition of St Basil setting out from Constantinople. No doubt Leo XIII's decision in 1880 was a way of making a similar point: he began the quest for better relations with the Orthodox Churches. But in the meantime, Europe has been divided into competing political and ideological systems. John Paul, like de Gaulle, believes in a *Europe des patries*, stretching from the Atlantic to the Urals. He will not therefore accept the EEC's usurpation of the adjective 'European', for that would imply that Poland was irretrievably lost to Western influence.

Frequently he speaks as much as a Slav as a Pole. Stimulated by his interest in these matters, the Lateran University in Rome and the Catholic University of Lublin in Poland co-sponsored a conference on 'The Christian Roots of the European Nations'. It took place in Rome in November 1981. 'Invited to the eternal city for four days of intensive activity,' said a breathless *L'Osservatore Romano*, 'were over two hundred intellectuals from twenty-three European and extra-European nations.' In his address to the conference, John Paul contrasted the Eastern and Western traditions in the following way:

> Benedict embraces the mainly Western and Central culture of Europe, which is more logical and rational . . . Cyril and Methodius highlight ancient Greek culture and the Eastern tradition, which is more mystical and intuitive. (6 November 1981)

It was precisely to bring out the complementary nature of East and West, John Paul explained, that at the start of 1981 he had declared Cyril and Methodius co-equal patrons of Europe alongside St Benedict. It was not that Benedict had been falling down on the job. The political consequences of this way of looking at the world will be explored later. Here it is enough to note that the attempt to strike a new balance between East and West, and the injection of a Slav element into the mainstream of Church life, is also seen as a compensation for centuries of neglect. Poles have felt misunderstood or abandoned by the West.

Once again, Iris Murdoch defined the problem with her usual precision – prophetic precision in this instance:

Everyone seemed to think of Poland, if thinking of it at all, in a sort of mechanical diplomatic sense as part of some more general problem: as a constituent of the Austro-Hungarian Empire, as one of the 'Eastern democracies'. The eternal 'Polish question' was never, it appeared, really about Poland at all, but about some use to which Poland could be put or some hindrance which Poland represented in the larger designs of others. No one seemed to perceive that unique burning flame of Polishness which though still dimmed by a ruthless neighbour continued to burn as it had always done. (*Nuns and Soldiers*, pp. 13–14)

Another novelist, Polish this time, has written that his compatriots sometimes behave 'as if the individual in Poland had no psychology of his own, as if there were only a national psychology' (Kazamierz Brandys, *A Question of Reality*, Charles Scribner's, New York, 1981, p. 19). As it stands, that is evident nonsense. John Paul cannot be reduced to being a specimen Pole. But anyone who wishes to understand him must start here and understand the historical resentments which haunt him.

He was just nineteen in 1939 when Poland was so brutally and so swiftly overwhelmed. The aim of the Nazi occupation of Poland was to destroy the intellectual élites and to turn the nation into a reservoir of slave labour. Karol Wojtyla went to work in the stone quarry. These experiences changed his life. They turned the poetry-writing, sport-loving, would-be actor into an intellectual priest of steely determination. In Brazil John Paul traced his priestly vocation directly to his wartime experiences. The horrors that he witnessed had convinced him that only spiritual remedies could overcome them. So whenever today John Paul echoes the language of Jacques Maritain and talks about 'the primacy of the spiritual', he is referring back to this fundamental experience. He stated this clearly in his address to the United Nations:

> Permit me to recall a constant rule of the history of humanity, a rule that is implicitly contained in all that I have already stated with regard to integral development and human rights. The rule is based on the relationship between spiritual and material or economic values. *In this relationship, it is the spiritual values that are pre-eminent*, both on account of the nature of those values and also for reasons concerning the good of man. (2 October 1979)

It would be difficult to make a more anti-Marxist statement than that. For Marxism had claimed to be 'the answer to the riddle of history' and to have discovered the 'law' that material relationships shape spiritual processes. John Paul stands Marx on his head.

There is, however, another aspect of his wartime experience that continues to affect him deeply: the closeness of Auschwitz. It is only seventeen miles from Wadowice where he was born and brought up, and only twenty-eight miles from Kraków where he spent most of his working life. He has referred to Auschwitz (which he always calls, very properly, by its Polish name, Oświecim) as 'this Golgotha of the modern world'. This was another theme he touched on in his address to the United Nations. For the experience of Oświecim is not over and done with. It is not just a frightening memory but it continues today:

> And everything that recalls those horrible experiences

should also disappear for ever from the lives of nations and states, everything that is *a continuation of those experiences under other forms*, namely the various kinds of torture and oppression, either physical or moral, carried out under *any system*, in any land; this phenomenon is all the more distressing if it occurs on the pretext of 'internal security' or the need to preserve an apparent peace. (2 October 1979)

Which countries did he have in mind? There seems no doubt that this was intended as an even-handed critique – of the type conducted by Amnesty International – directed against both the psychiatric prisons of the Soviet Union and the systematic torture in use in Latin American 'national security' states. And from 13 December 1981, Poland can be added to the list. What deepens the tragedy is the feeling that history is cyclic, that we have been here before.

So if a new Auschwitz or Oświecim is not just a past memory but a present reality, then we are all living on the edge of a volcano. This helps to explain the apocalyptic strain in the thinking of John Paul. For Oświecim represented evil on a gigantic, almost cosmic scale. Civilization is a thin veneer, easily pierced. The passion of Christ – a favourite Slav theme – continues in the sufferings of his brothers and sisters. Only if this suffering is accepted can it be transformed; and only then can the reality of the resurrection be glimpsed. This is not just a theory, any more than the heaped ashes and pathetic suitcases of Oświecim are a theory. For this truth had been embodied in the story of Fr Maximilian Kolbe, a forty-seven-year-old Franciscan, who sacrificed his life at Oświecim to save that of a married man.

It has been said that most people have their 'picture' of the world settled by about the age of twenty-five. By the time Karol Wojtyla was twenty-five, Kraków had been liberated, the truth about Oświecim had been fully disclosed, and another thing had happened to confirm his pessimism: the first atomic bomb was dropped on Hiroshima on 6 August 1945, Feast of the Transfiguration of the Lord. These events combined to give him a sense of life as an all-encompassing, life-or-death struggle between Good and Evil, God and the Devil. Evil can break through the thin crust of civilization at any moment. And this fundamental experience relativizes other questions. It makes it difficult for him to take seriously what we may call the 'liberal agenda' for the Church. Talk about birth control and women's ordination seems like distracting noises off, if the centre of the stage is fully occupied by the vast cosmic drama.

The word 'drama' frequently recurs in John Paul's mature style. It would be frivolous to link this with his brief acting career and his undoubted skills as an actor. It has more to do with his vision of the world as a battleground. He had this to say to the conference of 'The Christian Roots of Europe':

> The drama of sin and evil which, according to the gospel parable, sows fatal tares in the field of history, has weighed down terribly on Europe despite the message of great souls. And today the problem which harasses us is precisely *to save Europe and the world from further catastrophes*! (6 December 1981. Translation and italics from *L'Osservatore Romano*, English edition, 16 November 1981)

Which particular catastrophes? Certainly the possibility of nuclear annihilation is high on his list. He dispatched delegations from the Pontifical Academy of Sciences to world leaders, with grim warnings about the effects of nuclear war, in December 1981. But addressing another conference on 'The Crisis of the West and the Spiritual Task of Europe', he offered a variety of scenarios of catastrophe:

> Mankind as a whole is threatened by the possibility of atomic annihilation, as it is by explosive developments in

the third world which lead to catastrophic famine, the collapse of social and international structures as well as the spread of terrorism and violence. Uncontrolled industrial expansion and economic expansion endanger ecological balance, and the promotion of totalitarianism in new forms and by new methods poses new problems for the parliamentary democracies. (12 November 1981)

So scanning the international horizon, John Paul can see few grounds for hope.

John Paul's apocalyptic vision of human history, it is evident, is deeply pessimistic. On the last day of 1979 he went, according to tradition – Stendhal describes the same event in 1816 – to the Jesuit Church of the Gesù for the singing of the *Te Deum* in thanksgiving for all the graces of the year. But gloom prevailed over thanksgiving, and appeared to be gaining the upper hand. Commenting on 1 John 2:18 ('Many anti-Christs have appeared. My children, this is the last hour'), he said:

The evil which exists in the world, which encompasses and threatens man, nations and the whole of humanity, seems to be *greater than ever*, much greater than the evil for which each of us feels personally responsible. It is as though it grows within us according to its own inner dynamism and goes *far beyond human intentions*; as though it indeed came from us, but was not ours, according to the expression of the Apostle John. (31 December 1979)

Although John Paul went on in his homily to talk about Christ as the unconquerable light of the world, intuitive Slav pessimism seemed to prevail over rational Latin hope.

Having ended 1979 on this note, John Paul began 1980 in similar melancholy vein, spelling out in all their horrific consequences the results of a nuclear war: the death of 50 to 200 million people; a drastic reduction in the world's food supply owing to radio-activity; genetic mutations in the surviving human beings, as well as in the flora and fauna; changes in the atmosphere which would have unpredictable but certainly damaging consequences (1 January 1980). It was a doomsday scenario, detailed, unsparing, grisly, powerful as rhetoric. It was hardly balanced by the recommendation to search for 'reciprocal trust' and the prayer for 'peace to all men of good will'. One got the feeling that any development which appeared promising would turn out to be precarious. In *Familiaris Consortio* – John Paul's official response to the Synod on the family – there is a striking passage which sketches one particular type of contraceptive-user: 'Some ask themselves if it is a good thing to be alive or if it were better never to have been born; they doubt therefore if it is right to bring others into life when they will curse their existence in a cruel world with unforeseeable terrors' (No. 30). Such existentialist *Angst*, one thought, existed only in the novels of Dostoevsky. But John Paul has clearly encountered it in his Polish experience. From the age of twenty-five, he has been familiar with tragedy.

But hope, severely buffeted, never quite keeled over. Here is one memory, in his own words, from the year 1945:

I shall never forget the impression left with me by a Russian soldier. The war was only just over. A conscript knocked at the door of the Kraków seminary. When I asked, 'What is it you want?', he said that he wished to enter the seminary. Our conversation lasted a long time. Even though he never in fact entered – and incidentally was far from clear what a seminary really was – our meeting taught me, personally, one great truth: how wonderfully God succeeds in penetrating the human mind even in the extremely unfavourable conditions of the systematic denial of him. In the whole of his adult life that soldier had never gone inside a church. At school and then later at work, he had continually heard people saying 'There is no God'. And in spite of all that, he said more than once: 'But I always knew that God exists ... and now

I would like to learn something about him.' (*Sign of Contradiction*, St Paul Publications, Slough, 1979, p. 15. Translation modified)

At the time of this conversation, Karol Wojtyla was twenty-five and preparing for ordination.

3

Priests out of Politics

If being Polish is the most important fact about John Paul II, the second most important is that he is a Polish *priest*. The following remark to the young French people gathered at Parc des Princes is typical: 'I've been pope for nearly two years, a bishop for over twenty years, but for me the most important thing is still that I am a priest' (1 June 1980). He meant that the power to celebrate Mass and to give absolution – the definition of the priest according to the Council of Trent – were what counted most for him. That was why on the morning of Good Friday, 1980, astonished penitents found the Pope in a confessional box in St Peter's, 'exercising his priesthood'. One can say that his concept of the papacy is in continuity with his concept of the priesthood: both are instances of sacramental ministry that set the priest apart and give him special status in the community. It is no accident that the Polish word for 'prince' (*kiąże*) is linked with the word for 'priest' (*ksądz*).

Yet young Karol Wojtyla could so easily have been a different kind of priest – a 'religious' priest as opposed to a diocesan priest (what was called at the time, a 'secular priest'). He was greatly drawn to the Carmelites. His Roman thesis at the Angelicum University was on 'The Concept of Faith in the Writings of St John of the Cross'. It was this Carmelite poet who had talked of 'the dark night of the senses' and, still more mysteriously, of 'the dark night of the soul' as the necessary purification through which the Christian, in his pilgrim's progress, had to go before he would be fit to encounter God. After the experience of wartime Poland, the choice of subject for his thesis explains itself. How could faith survive the dark night of the Polish soul?

The Vicar General of Kraków, Bishop Julian Groblicki, has explained that although Wojtyla thought of becoming a Carmelite, he was told by his spiritual director, '*Ad majores res tu es*' – 'You are made for greater things'. It sounds like worldly advice from a man of God. But Wojtyla accepted it. Yet he never lost the Carmelite and St John of the Cross sense of the pregnant paradoxes of faith: God is the darkness that illumines, the music that is soundless, the poem that is wordless. If John Paul is sometimes hard to follow, it may be because he has wandered away into these mystic regions.

The Franciscan influence was also strong. The example of Maximilian Kolbe has already been mentioned. He was the exemplar of the priest as the 'Good Shepherd', who is prepared to lay down his life for his flock. He was devoted to Our Lady. He was, like Christ, a 'man for others'. A large statue of Kolbe stands in the crypt of the new church at Nowa Huta near Kraków. He wears the striped garb of Auschwitz. He remains for John Paul the chief near-contemporary exemplar of the priest. And he is as far away from the Latin American models of the 'liberation theology' priest as can be imagined.

But in the end young Karol Wojtyla chose neither the Carmelites nor the Franciscans. He became a diocesan priest in Kraków. Undoubtedly one of his 'models' for the priesthood was Prince Prince Adam Sapieha – so styled because he was a prince by birth and a prince of the Church. In the summer of 1938, a month before Wojtyla's matriculation, he came to present the prizes at the gymnasium in Wadowice. The eighteen-year-old gave an elegant and well-turned speech of welcome. The rest of the story comes from Fr Edward Zacher, still parish priest in Wadowice at the time of the 1978 conclave:

> The Archbishop was very impressed. He turned to me and looking at Lolek (Karol's nickname) asked: 'Do you think

we could ever make a priest of him?' 'I don't know,' I replied, 'he's in love with the theatre and they've talked him into reading Polish literature at the university.' 'A very great pity,' said Sapieha, 'we need someone like him.' (George Blazynski, *John Paul II, A Man from Krakow*, p. 37)

When, a decade later, Fr Wojtyla began to read Max Scheler, the German phenomenologist, he discovered the theory of the importance of 'models' and 'examples' in the moral life. It matched his own experience in coming to the priesthood. He was not starting from scratch. He was inserted into a living tradition.

So we can pause for a moment and dwell on the figure of Sapieha. Born in 1867 he had studied theology at Innsbruck in Austria, where the Jesuits had charge of the theological faculty. The young prince-seminarians of the Austro-Hungarian Empire cut a dashing figure as they rode round Innsbruck in their national costume, followed by a suite of servants and sometimes a private chaplain. Sapieha worked in the Vatican, 1903–14, during the worst years of the anti-Modernist campaign. Inevitably he became a Bishop in 1912.

He moved back to Kraków in 1914 and devoted himself to charitable works during the First World War. As a patriotic Pole he welcomed the new and independent Poland that came into being with the armistice of 1918. In 1920 the Polish Bishops met at Czestochowa to discuss the post-war situation. They had forgotten to inform the papal representative in Poland who, nevertheless, turned up on the doorstep. Sapieha sent him away, carefully explaining that this was a meeting of *Polish* Bishops which did not require the presence of the man from Rome. The trouble was that the Apostolic Visitor, thus rebuffed, was none other than Achille Ratti, who within two years was to become Pope Pius XI. He never forgot or forgave Sapieha, and later banned prelates from being members of parliament. Many believed that this ban was directed against Sapieha, who sat in the Polish Sejm as a member of the National Democratic Party. Both incidents confirm that any notion that relationships between the Polish Bishops and the Vatican were always characterized by sweetness and light, is a myth. Trouble was never far away.

So it was Sapieha who welcomed Karol Wojtyla into his household in 1942. By now he was seventy-five, but still erect and fearless. But in his single recorded meeting with the Nazi military governor, Hans Frank, on 5 May 1944 he behaved ambiguously, calling the work of the partisans murder and shamefully attributing some of the attacks on the Germans to Jews (cf. George Huntston Williams, *The Mind of John Paul II*, Seabury Press, New York, 1981, pp. 81–8). Like most Poles of his generation, the fine balance of his detestation came down more firmly against communists. It was Sapieha who decided to send Wojtyla to Rome in 1946 – a courageous and imaginative decision at a time when the country was painfully rebuilding. In that same year he was, very belatedly, made a cardinal (he had been Archbishop of Kraków since 1925), but haughtily refused to wear his crimson robes. 'I shall not wear them,' he said, 'so long as my country is suffering.' He died in 1951. The memorial plaque on his tomb in the Franciscan church opposite his – later Wojtyla's – residence, is inscribed with the words: 'Prayer in the Dark Night of Occupation'.

Of course Wojtyla was no carbon-copy of his archbishop, but he did take a great deal from him. They have in common toughness, the feeling that a Polish Bishop must act for the good of the nation – though where the good lies may be difficult to decide – an inability to suffer fools, especially clerical fools, gladly, an instinctive populism, and a traditional idea of the priesthood in which concepts such as honour and fidelity are as important as that of service.

The priest who emerges from this tradition is a hero figure, rather like the Abbé Donissan in Georges Bernanos's novel, *Sous le Soleil de Satan* (Plon, Paris, 1926). He is a spiritual athlete, a champion who on behalf of the whole community engages in single-handed combat with the evil one. The apocalyptic context described in the previous chapters reinforces the idea that the priest is supremely tested, supremely vulnerable and supremely triumphant. Addressing religious priests at Altötting, a Marian shrine in West Germany, John Paul said:

> You are called to share in a special way in this spiritual struggle. You are called to this constant combat that Mother Church is engaged upon and which fashions it into the image of the Woman, the Mother of the Lord. You have at the heart of your vocation the adoration of Holy God; but by the same token you are particularly exposed to the temptations of the Evil One, as is evident in the temptations of the Lord. (18 November 1980)

Here the priest or religious is seen as someone at the point of intersection between Good and Evil, and his soul is a battleground between God and Satan. This is why John Paul does not take kindly to those priests who wish to withdraw from the battlefield. He finds their position inconceivable and dishonourable. He thinks of them as deserters.

There is and can be no higher vocation than that to the priesthood. Though John Paul admits, in his Maundy Thursday Letter to Priests in 1979, that 'the common priesthood of the faithful' exists, he draws no conclusions from this doctrine. And he insists on the difference between the 'common priesthood' of all the baptized and the 'hierarchical priesthood' of the ordained. They are said to differ 'essentially and not only in degree'. This obscure phrase is repeated three times. Moreover, the priest, 'essentially different', is dropped down on the people he has to serve, as it were by parachute. For the priesthood, he writes, 'does not take its origin from the community as though it were the community that "called" or "delegated" him' (No. 4). This is the gist of what John Paul has to say about the priesthood. He has repeated it innumerable times on his international journeys. The priesthood is from above. Therefore the particular needs of the community, the lack of priests, the desire of women to be ordained, are all totally irrelevant because the present organization of the ministry represents a final stage in the development of theology.

This is a defensible view. But it is also one-sided. It involves the choice of a particular theological approach. At the 1971 Synod, which was devoted in part to this theme, Bishop Santos Ascarza of Chile outlined the two contrasting methods:

> The first starts from scripture and the priesthood of Christ in order to determine the purpose, scope and meaning of the priestly ministry once for all [*semel pro semper*] and then proceeds to draw appropriate conclusions for our time. It is clear but abstract. The other method starts from the 'signs of the times', the crisis in the priesthood and the conditions in which the apostolate is today developing, and then discerns what Christ is asking of us today. (Cf. Peter Hebblethwaite, *The Runaway Church*, Fount Paperbacks, 1978[2], p. 62)

The two methods, which may be called deductive (from first principles) or inductive (from experience), do not give the same results. Cardinal Wojtyla had correctly perceived the dangers which might result from the inductive method: it would become more difficult, for example, to hold the line against the ordination of women or married men, since the argument 'it has never been done before' is strictly irrelevant to the question, 'What is God asking of us today?' John Paul sticks to the well-trodden path of the deductive method.

The real importance of the 1971 Synod – though few noticed it there and then – was that for the first time a Germano-Polish alliance emerged and began to show its strength. On the German side the leader was Cardinal Joseph Höffner of Cologne, aided by the Swiss theologian Hans Urs von Balthasar. Poland was represented by

Cardinal Karol Wojtyla. Their general purpose was to counteract 'progressive' interpretations of the Council found, for example, in the review *Concilium*, and in theologians such as Edward Schillebeeckx and Hans Küng. Their particular goal, in 1971, was to stop a semantic shift from 'ministerial priesthood' towards 'priestly ministry' (the term used in the draft text for the Synod). The alliance approved of the 'ministerial priesthood' because it kept everything as it was. But they had correctly seen the danger of talking about 'priestly ministry': it implied that there were other forms of ministry – catechetics, healing, teaching, even administration – which might stand alongside and complement the *priestly* ministry. But then the priestly ministry would have lost its uniqueness and become one ministry among others. The Germano-Polish alliance just won the battle of the 1971 Synod. It was a remote preparation for the second conclave of 1978 and foreshadowed the pontificate of John Paul II.

John Paul always presents his views on the priesthood as though they were 'out of time'; but they are strongly rooted in the particular Polish tradition. One can form a good idea of this Polish context from Adam Boniecki, a priest of the diocese of Kraków, who is at present in Rome as the editor of the Polish edition of *L'Osservatore Romano*. It would be difficult to find a more reliable and respectable source. Boniecki contributed a chapter on Polish priests to *Nous Chrétiens de Pologne* (Cana, Paris, 1979). He makes three points about priests in Poland that are relevant to our theme.

The first is that priests do not quarrel with their Bishops. 'There is not, and cannot be,' he writes, 'any contestation in the Polish Church.' This idyll does not come about because Polish priests are any more virtuous than others. It is a product of the embattled state of the Church. In a 'life or death' situation, any hint of dissent will be self-censored by the potential dissident if not suppressed by the Bishop. Despite the development – up to 13 December 1981 – of

Solidarity, there have been no priestly councils in Poland and no democratic procedures. John Paul has mentioned diocesan and priestly councils only once: it was in the conclusion to the Dutch Synod and he said they should not resemble trades unions. This emphasis on uniformity helps to explain John Paul's distaste, indeed incomprehension, when faced by what he regards as 'dissident' priests or religious. He takes decisive action. He is insensitive to the argument that a totally united hierarchy is an incredible myth that can only be purchased at the price of suppressing differences. He told the German Bishops at Fulda that it was nonsense to suppose that making public their divisions would make them more credible. Unity is all. Or the façade of unity. This is why John Paul prefers Bishops to have private meetings and then announce their unanimous conclusions afterwards.

So Polish priests are docile and obedient. Or if they are not, they depart on tiptoe. Boniecki reports that one priest friend of his preferred to resign from the priesthood because he could not, in conscience, impose the strict letter of *Humanae Vitae* on his inadequately housed people. How many priests in the West have done the same?

Boniecki's third relevant point concerns priests who wish to resign. It had better be given in his own words:

> For other colleagues the decisive problem was celibacy. Public opinion treats very badly a priest who leaves the ministry. It favours clerical celibacy. Nobody proclaims publicly a departure. It is rather concealed as though it were something shameful. (ibid., p. 138)

These are exactly the assumptions that lay behind John Paul's 'Norms for Laicization' (27 October 1980) which replaced Paul VI's relatively compassionate Norms (13 January 1971). The request for laicization is now regarded as a disgrace and a confession of failure. The procedure has been made as difficult as possible. A priest can only be dispensed if he can demonstrate that he was invalidly ordained: he might, for instance, have been coerced into ordination by his Breton grandmother. But he has to be able to find witnesses with whom he talked about this coercion. The only other possibility is that 'after some time' a priest who 'seeks to rectify a situation from which he cannot free himself' (that is Vaticanese for having a wife and children) *may* be dispensed. But that presupposes that he first put himself in an uncanonical situation and must therefore cut himself off from the Church. Some will face a dilemma: hypocrisy or irregularity.

Cardinal Franjo Seper's letter accompanying the new norms said that 'the widespread diffusion of this phenomenon' (i.e. laicization) 'has inflicted a painful blow on the Church'. One would like to know the evidence for that statement: there is only a 'painful blow' if one starts out from the presuppositions expressed by Fr Boniecki. John Paul shares them. But they are not universal.

John Paul's model priest is male, celibate, committed for life, dressed in clerical black, docile, prayerful, holy, apolitical, if need be heroic. His Maundy Thursday 1979 letter to priests spelled it all out in detail. His apologists were so dumbfounded by it that they invented the fantastic tale that the conclave had drawn up some such document and imposed it on a reluctant pope.

Nothing could be further from the truth. Style and content proved that it was all his own work. He was continuing the line he had defended at the 1971 Synod. Moreover, John Paul is a combative man who always replies to critics. 'Here and there,' he told a meeting of Polish priests at Czestochowa, 'it has been suggested that the Pope was trying to impose the Polish model of the priesthood on the whole world. But these were isolated voices looking for something that was not there.' So the anonymous critics were simply brushed aside. But then, astonishingly, John Paul conceded the whole case: 'I came away from Poland in the deep conviction that it was only with this vision of the priesthood that the Church would survive' (6 June 1979. Quoted by Nicholas Carroll in *The Pope from Poland*, edited by John Whale, Collins, 1980, p. 155. The official version of the speech, as it appears in *Return to Poland*, Collins, 1979, pp. 103–5, does not contain these remarks. But I trust Carroll's cassette recorder more than the editors of *L'Osservatore Romano*).

To put it quite simply, John Paul believed that there was a crisis of identity in the priesthood which he has now resolved. As a result, vocations will begin to pick up again and the seminaries will be filled. Any evidence that this could just possibly be beginning to be verified, is eagerly seized upon.

He also believed that there was a crisis of identity among religious men and women. Here we are concerned only with religious priests. Some religious orders think that John Paul underestimates the importance of their autonomy, fails to appreciate their originality and special 'charism' (or founder's grace), and wants to reduce them to being subordinates of the bishop. This tendency found its most striking expression in the appointment of 'a personal delegate of the Holy Father to the Society of Jesus' in October 1981. It was difficult not to see this as a disavowal of the policies and methods used by the ousted General, Fr Pedro Arrupe, who had been in charge since 1964. Arrupe's resignation had not been accepted, not even after a stroke had incapacitated him in August 1981. The appointment of a delegate meant that the Jesuits could not be trusted to organize a General Congregation to elect a new General.

This mistrust of religious has deep roots. The Council of the Synod, which met 24–27 October 1972, had to decide the theme for the forthcoming Synod. Many suggestions had been received from episcopal conferences around the world. Cardinal Wojtyla suggested *De Vita Religiosa – On Religious Life*. This was not adopted because no one else had thought it an urgent matter. But Wojtyla was sufficiently intent on his project to draft a brief text in Latin which showed how deeply concerned he already was.

He began by saying that this theme is of the greatest importance and that religious life is in a state of *crisis*. The evidence is crisply summarized: 'Defections; lack of vocations; infidelity in keeping the vows.' The second paragraph proposed remedies based on the principle of 'a better insertion in the present-day mission of the Church'. He suggested that this 'better insertion' should happen both on the level of the universal Church (by which religious orders are linked to the papacy) and on the level of the local church (by which religious are linked to the bishop). To achieve this 'better insertion' he said that there should be a study of the concept of 'exemption' – the juridical device which enables some religious orders to be less dependent on the local bishops in order to be more directly related to the pope (*Karol Wojtyla e il Sinodo dei Vescovi*, Vatican Press, 1980, p. 127).

Thus as Archbishop of Kraków he thought that religious needed bringing under firmer control. As Pope he has made a start with the Jesuits, who are not only the largest religious order (26,653 at the last count) but the most intellectually influential. They will now have to put their house in order – though no one quite knows what this will mean in detail. It seems that they are being blamed for theological adventurousness, political involvement, especially in Latin America, and the hold-all charge of 'secularization'. Though the Jesuits are at the moment in the front line, by taking them on John Paul has served notice on other orders – such as Dominicans and Franciscans – that they had better reform themselves or steps will be taken to reform them.

It has been said several times in this chapter that John Paul holds that priests should be apolitical. This may seem surprising in view of his own and Cardinal Stefan Wyszyński's activity in Poland. And Archbishop Glemp, Wyszyński's successor, has carried on in the same tradition. He has warned and pleaded and negotiated with the government and written to all the members of the Sejm (the Polish Parliament). On any definition, he has acted politically. But in the Polish system one has apolitical priests, while the prelates are heavily engaged in politics. This paradox, a very Polish one, will be explored in the next chapter.

4

Prelates in Politics

What constitutes being 'in' or 'not in' politics is often a matter of argument. Sometimes the suggestion that 'priests should stay clear of politics' is merely another way of saying that they should support the (probably unjust) *status quo*. In Poland there has long been a tradition that the Primate should act as *inter-rex*, the regent who governed the country in the absence of a king. Cardinal Stefan Wyszyński entered into this inheritance, quite naturally. After emerging from house arrest in 1956, he lectured the government on every possible occasion. A stream of advice, exhortation and condemnation flowed from his vigorous pen. Archbishop Glemp, right from the start, took the same approach, encouraged by Pope John Paul II.

Why, then, this paradoxical insistence that 'priests should keep out of politics' when manifestly prelates do not? The answer is partly a semantic point. Until Solidarity began to turn the place upside down, political life in Poland meant the life of the Communist Party (or, strictly speaking, the Polish United Workers' Party). It was the only manifestation of political activity that had government approval. So keeping out of politics was another way of keeping out of activities sponsored by the Communist Party. Some misguided priests joined the pro-government Pax movement and so were inveigled into 'politics': they were denounced by the Bishops as dupes or opportunists.

Bishops had the same reasons for 'keeping out of politics'. But on the other hand they had responsibility for the fate of the nation and the common good of its citizens. This was the ground on which they stood. This was the basis on which they could denounce the government as failing the nation and the people. And since the unity of the episcopate was the condition of their effectiveness, the Cardinal Primate and whatever other cardinals there happened to be, concentrated in themselves the authority of the entire episcopal conference. They did not believe that they were 'interfering in politics' when they addressed themselves to the good of the nation, because the nation was (fairly permanently) in crisis, and because the Bishops embodied its conscience.

It is merely inept not to call this a form of political commitment, although one also has to concede that it is *more* than a mere political commitment. John Paul learned about these things in the Polish context before he stepped on to the world stage. He carried over attitudes shaped in Poland into his new task as pope. We can best discover what this means by considering what happened when he went back home to Poland in 1979. He was now, beyond any doubt, 'the world's most famous Pole'. He added the prestige of his office to the power of his personality. During the visit he exercised four interrelated 'roles' (to use the jargon of political theorists), each of them thoroughly political.

In the first place he appeared as the advocate of a counter-culture, an alternative society, based on the long intertwining of Church and nation in Polish history. When they met in the Belvedere Palace, Mr Edward Gierek, not yet dismissed and disgraced, spoke routinely of the achievements of thirty-five years of socialism. In reply John Paul pointedly ignored these achievements, which are indeed difficult to detect, and spoke instead of the more than a thousand-year-old tradition of Poland. He was implicitly contrasting the *pays légal*, which was communist, with the *pays réel*, which is Catholic. With that slightly malicious wit of which he is capable, he congratulated Mr Gierek on rebuilding, not quite with his own hands, the Royal Palace in Warsaw, 'as a symbol of Polish sovereignty'. It was done with feline politeness. Gierek could hardly complain, as the branch on which he had been sitting was neatly and efficiently sawn off.

Secondly, John Paul acted as a 'tribune of the people'. A bishop or a cardinal grows in authority in Poland if he can put into words what people are feeling but dare not say. In Victory Square, Warsaw, on 2 June 1979, his homily was interrupted for more than ten minutes when he said: 'Christ cannot be kept out of the history of man in any part of the globe. The exclusion of Christ from history is an act against man.' At this there were chants of 'We want God! We want God!' which had the precise rhythms of a football crowd. It was an extraordinary moment in the capital of a communist country, where atheism is officially inculcated from the nursery school to the university. Yet John Paul had done nothing very difficult. He had simply articulated what most Poles believe. And he had done so in the square which summed up so much of Polish history: here Napoleon had reviewed his troops before setting off on his Russian Campaign; here the Cossacks had charged the weeping crowd when a statue of Adam Mickiewicz was unveiled in 1863; here the Nazis had put up an enormous and short-lived concrete V to mark their conquest of the Soviet Union; and here was the tomb of the Polish unknown soldier.

In this setting John Paul had simply spoken the truth – and the earth had not opened to swallow him up. It was then that Solidarity – or its equivalent – became possible and likely. John Paul had shown his fellow Poles that the bluff of the regime could be called, that perfect order could be kept without the use of force or the militia, and that if the people were freely allowed to choose their government, it would not be that of Edward Gierek. In that way the visit to Poland acted as a kind of informal plebiscite. It was also 'destabilizing' in the sense of potentially upsetting the *status quo*. And John Paul knew perfectly well what he was doing.

Yet at the same time he did not behave as a demagogue who merely flatters people by telling them what they want to know. As 'tribune of the people', he also behaved responsibly. He incited no one to rebellion. He treated the 'civil authorities' with the utmost civility – even thanking the police for looking after him. But in exchange for this 'moderation', he hoped that the Church would be able to secure better conditions for itself in negotiations with the state. This was John Paul's third role in Poland: he appeared as a 'realist' with a 'sense of the possible'. This was the note he struck in his address to the Polish Bishops in Czestochowa:

> We are aware that the dialogue [between Church and state] cannot be easy, because it takes place between two concepts of the world that are diametrically opposed. But it must be made possible and effective since the good of individuals and the nation demands it. (5 June 1979)

The context makes it plain that the 'dialogue' envisaged here is not a process in which the Church expects to learn anything. It is not an intellectual exchange at all. It is rather a negotiation from a position of moral strength, from which the Church hopes to gain certain rights – access to the media, freedom to build new churches, legally ratified property rights. In return the Church will not seek to overthrow the government. That is a modest enough concession, and does not reveal any great enthusiasm for 'the building of socialism'. But that, in any case, is ruled out, since 'the two concepts of the world are diametrically opposed'.

This tough-minded realism implied that there would be a long war of attrition, unless the link between 'socialism' and the ideology which underpins it was weakened or dissolved. In the end the ideology of socialism proved to be made of cardboard: one serious push and it was broken through. But then the geo-political realities of the situation – the fact that the Soviet Union is next door – asserted themselves, and 'socialism' was reimposed by force of arms.

The fourth role, finally, is that of prophet or visionary. At the tomb of St Adalbert, the Czech who in the tenth century went to convert the Baltic peoples at the invitation of King Bodeslaw the Brave, John Paul prayed for Slavs everywhere.

He wondered aloud whether God had not chosen him, the first Polish Pope, to bring a special Slav witness to the world: 'Is not the Holy Spirit disposed to see that this Polish Pope, this Slav Pope, should at this very moment reveal the spiritual unity of Europe?' (Gniezno, 3 June 1979). In that setting it was an astonishing claim to make. All the Slav peoples are within the Soviet 'sphere of influence' – but only by a temporary aberration of history, John Paul seemed to be saying. Does this mean that he believes that 'the spiritual unity of Europe', expressed inchoately in and through the Church, can and should be matched by actual political unity? I think he does, though in God's own time and according to his mysterious ways.

This is another instance of the 'primacy of the spiritual' that means so much to him. First get your thinking right, and change in the practical order will follow. To talk of 'the spiritual unity of Christian Europe' is to ignore the frontiers on the map and to think instead of those 'frontiers of the mind' of which he spoke in the last article written before he became Pope. So for him the Easternmost boundary of Europe is not a traceable line on the map but rather 'the frontier of the penetration of the Gospel and secondly the frontier of invasions coming from Asia'. No one quite knows where that is. But John Paul offered two criteria for determining where it might be. He asked of the peoples of this frontier region: 'To what extent is their sense of humanity and the dignity of man derived from the Gospel? Where does servile passivity, derived from centuries of slavery, begin?' The answer to the second question is: 'Certainly not in Poland.'

All this has two important consequences for John Paul's judgements on international affairs. The first is that his defence of 'human rights', which is constant and unambiguous, is not based on the two great 'Enlightenment' statements on the subject which are contained in the American Declaration of Independence of 1776 and the French Revolutionary Declaration on the rights of man in 1789. His defence of human rights does not have a secular origin. It is based on the Gospel.

The second consequence is that the distinction between 'state' and 'nation' comes easily and spontaneously to him. His parents, he has frequently pointed out, had the passport of a foreign state (the Austro-Hungarian Empire) while belonging to the Polish nation. For in the partition of Poland in the nineteenth century, while the Polish 'state' had ceased to exist, the 'nation' survived, its sense of identity preserved by the unbreakable alliance between Church, language and culture. In this way the distinction between 'nation' and 'state' becomes almost the equivalent of that between '*le pays réel*' and '*le pays légal*'. In Polish experience the 'state' has often been a tyrannical imposition. And in preferring the 'nation' John Paul is making an appeal to the 'people' over the heads of the provisional rulers of the state. The roots of his instinctive 'populism' lie here.

John Paul does not hesitate to apply the lessons learned in Poland to the whole world. In his address to UNESCO in Paris on 2 June 1980 (almost exactly one year after his 'spiritual unity of Europe' speech in Gniezno), he urged the delegates to protect and cherish the nation 'as the apple of your eye' (No. 15). Knowing that for many of his hearers the idea of 'nation' had been tarnished because of its association with 'nationalism', he directly appealed to his Polish experience as the source and vindication of his theory of the nation:

The nation is the community that has a history which surpasses the history of the individual or the family . . . In everything I am now saying, my words come from a particular experience and are a *special witness*. I am the son of a nation that has undergone many experiences in history, a nation that has been condemned to death by its neighbours several times, and yet which has remained itself. It preserved its identity and, despite partitions and countless occupations, its national sovereignty, not by relying on physical strength but solely by *relying on culture*. (No. 15, 2 June 1980)

In John Paul's vision of the world, the Polish experience is exemplary.

The immediate political consequence of laying stress on the nation is that it provides the grounds for denouncing any 'interference in the affairs of another country', whoever is doing the interfering. In Poland he denounced imperialism, whether military, economic or political: and everyone knew that he was talking about 'the friendly neighbour to the East'. But the same remark was repeated in Africa, where it became an exhortation to the super-powers to stay out of the continent. It has been used in connection with the Lebanon, where it is a courteous way of urging the Syrians to go home. It has also made John Paul sympathetic towards the Palestinians, another 'people' without a 'state'. He takes seriously the traditional slogan of Polish revolutionaries: 'For our freedom and yours.'

John Paul is the most novel and arresting figure to have appeared on the international scene in the last decade. The competition is not keen: ageing and lack-lustre politicians occupy the stage. Young people, in East and West, have lost faith in official bureaucracies, because they have become remote from everyday human experience. The Pope, on the other hand, attracts them because he speaks the same language as all the unofficial movements – press campaigns for human rights, support for Soviet dissidents and for Solidarity, the Nobel peace prizes, Amnesty International, the anti-nuclear movement – which have perceptibly changed the international atmosphere. In the blah-blah of conventional politics, John Paul speaks a language that is direct, authentic and manifestly sincere.

What he has done, in fact, is to extend to the whole world the four 'roles' he learned in Poland. He tells the world that there is an alternative society, founded on love, justice and brotherhood. He acts as the 'tribune of the people' in that he systematically becomes 'the voice of those who have no voice' and puts into words the aspirations of the oppressed and the marginalized. At the same time he is realistic in that he does not expect Utopia to come tomorrow. And he retains a vision, a dream: that of a civilization built on love and trust. In his first and most moving message for World Peace Day he wrote: 'Leaders of the nations and of the international organizations will have to learn to find a new language, a language of peace: of its very nature it will create new room for peace' (1 January 1979). Creating space: abolishing frontiers: opening doors that are shut. These are not only the dominant images used by John Paul; they express what the Church may be expected to contribute to what one is compelled to call . . . international politics.

All of which is perfectly admirable. But there remain one or two quibbles which candour compels one to set down. The first was well put by Paul Thibaud, writing in *Esprit*, the French 'personalist' review which has always been influential in Poland. Thibaud remarked that the Polish Bishops were in a unique position: 'They have immense moral influence, but no actual responsibility. If things go wrong, it is always somebody else's fault, never the Church's' (*Esprit*, March 1979). This observation can be applied to the pontificate. If John Paul exhorts the nations to recognize human rights, he does not speak about human rights within the Church. He dispatches members of the Pontifical Academy of Sciences to the United Nations, to Presidents Ronald Reagan, Leonid Brezhnev, François Mitterand and to Mrs Margaret Thatcher, in order to acquaint them with the appalling consequences of unleashing a nuclear war and to prompt them to immediate multi-lateral disarmament, but the Pope himself has no nuclear weapons to renounce. He urged President João Figueiredo of Brazil to implement 'speedy reforms', but gave him a loop-hole by adding that this was the only way to prevent them being sought 'under the influence of ideological systems that do not hesitate to have recourse to violence and the suppression of liberty and the rights that are fundamental to the dignity of man' (13 June 1980). In other words, reform now, or reap the Marxist whirlwind later. This may sound like common sense. But the truth is that, as the Brazilian Bishops have repeatedly pointed out, the regime of President Figueiredo is characterized by 'violence and the suppression of liberty and the rights that are fundamental to the dignity of man'. It is difficult to understand why right-wing dictators – President Marcos of the Philippines would be another example – are treated with greater indulgence and leniency than left-wing dictators. The difference is that the former tend to claim to be 'Catholics'. John Paul's apparently successful mediation between Chile and the Argentine, though welcome in that it prevented war, was dangerous in so far as it seemed to imply that these two military dictatorships were shining examples of 'Catholic nations' who might be expected to invoke the mediation of the Pope.

The second quibble is that John Paul's Polish experience has left him with a profound scepticism about Marxism which is not shared by all Catholics. Pedro Arrupe put a rope around his own neck when he wrote a letter to the Jesuits of Latin America suggesting that it was possible, though extremely difficult, to make a distinction between Marxism as an analysis of the forces at work in society (which might be illuminating) and Marxism as a philosophy (which was always to be sternly rejected). In this way Arrupe sealed his fate. Because John Paul comes from a communist country, he believes that he is an expert on Marxism. In his experience, and in the Polish experience generally, the total discrepancy between theory and practice dispenses him from taking Marxism seriously. It is simply wrong. In Chapter 3 of his major philosophical work, *The Acting Person* (The Yearbook of Phenomenological Research, Vol. X, D. Reidel, Dordrecht, Holland, 1979), he dismisses Marxism in a single tart phrase. The chapter is devoted to 'The personal structure of self-determination', referring to freedom and its correlative, responsibility. Determinism in its Marxist form is dispatched with the comment that 'a certain preconception of matter tends to intervene in the interpretation of the person rather than allow experience to present all its evidence to the end' (ibid., p. 133). On this topic the reader is advised to consult 'any suitable treatise or handbook'. This explains why John Paul is so ready to dismiss the Latin American 'theology of liberation'. It has felt the heady appeal of Marxism. But for him it is an ideology which contaminates the Gospel and not, as for Chesterton and Paul VI, 'a Christian idea gone wrong'.

The third and final quibble concerns the difficulty of making Poland an exemplary nation. John Paul clearly believes that Poland is *The Key to Europe* (according to the title of a book he quotes by L. S. Buell, which appeared in 1940). But Poland's particular fusion of culture and Catholicism is found nowhere else. True, John Paul has tried in vain to rekindle it in France, which is why he could conclude his sermon at Le Bourget airport with the anachronistic apostrophe: 'France, eldest daughter of the Church, are you faithful to your baptismal promises?' He also tried to present Brazil and the Philippines as essentially 'Catholic nations'. Faced with the problem of Germany, whose national consciousness has been shaped as much by Lutheranism as by Catholicism, he invented an 'image' of Germany in which only its Catholic past had a place. In Japan, even this resource failed, and he was obliged to fall back on the 'remarkable natural virtues' found in the Japanese national tradition.

In short, although Poland can provide a unique, always interesting and often illuminating perspective on international affairs, it does have its limitations. These limitations can be seen, for example, in the Polish attitude to the Second Vatican Council.

5

Interpreting the Council

The Second Vatican Council (1962–5) was the most important event in the life of the Roman Catholic Church in this century. It acted as a watershed. Special terms were used to denote 'before' and 'after' the Council, pre-conciliar and post-conciliar, and it was understood that they pointed to a difference in attitudes as much as to a chronological difference. Of course it would be absurd to imagine the Council as a sort of wonder-working pill which could of itself transform the Church in a quasi-magical manner. But it made a difference to all the roles and tasks in the Church, to its self-understanding and to its relationships with other Christians, other faiths and the world generally. For this reason the question most urgently asked after John Paul's surprise election was: is he committed to the Council?

He answered this question in his first major address and answered it positively:

> We consider our primary duty to be that of promoting, with prudent but encouraging action, the most exact fulfilment of the norms and directives of the Council. Above all we must favour the development of conciliar attitudes. First one must be in harmony with the Council. One must put into effect what was stated in its documents; and what was 'implicit' should be made explicit in the light of the experiments that followed and in the light of new emerging circumstances. (17 October 1978)

The last sentence was particularly significant: it seems to imply a kind of 'continued Council'. Most curial conservatives considered that the period of 'experiment' was long over. This was therefore a bold and 'progressive' statement.

But how *personal* was this address to the college of cardinals delivered on the day after his election? However rapid one's thought processes and adept one's pen, it does seem rather unlikely that on the night one has been elected the first Slav pope in history, one can calmly sit down and compose a discourse of this length and substance. John Paul was helped, if only to translate the text into Latin. But the address was the result of the pre-conclave deliberations on 'the kind of pope' the cardinals felt the Church needed. And they wanted someone who was firmly committed to Vatican II. Cardinal Giuseppe Siri, a rival candidate, was not so committed. Cardinal Karol Wojtyla was.

But the new Pope did manage to contribute some personal touches to the prepared text. It came out in his fascination – obsession would not be too strong a word – with the year AD 2000. He saw the Church as on a pilgrim journey towards an open future: 'What is the fate the Lord has in store for his Church in the next years? And what path will humanity take as it draws near to the year 2000? These are difficult questions, to which we can only reply: God knows' (17 October 1978). That left room for hope.

So John Paul's commitment to the Council appeared firm and definitive. But what did it really mean, and how would it be 'cashed'? It ought, in principle, to be relatively easy to discover what Cardinal Wojtyla thought about the Council since he devoted a whole book to it: *Sources of Renewal* (Collins and Fount Paperbacks, 1980. The original Polish edition came out in 1972). But *Sources of Renewal* is a disappointing work, and the fact that John Paul hesitated to have it republished does credit to his judgement.

Much of it consists of long quotations from the sixteen Council documents. This could be justified on the grounds that there was still no cheap popular edition of the Council documents available in Poland. So part of Wojtyla's task was simply to transcribe and make known texts that had been readily available elsewhere for over six years. The author explains that his book is not a commentary on the documents of Vatican II, but rather 'a vade-mecum introducing the reader to these documents, but always from the point of view of translating them into the life of the Church'. So his aim was practical and pastoral.

But we can define the purpose of *Sources of Renewal* even more precisely. It was written as a 'working paper' for the Synod of the diocese of Kraków which, because of the special circumstances of Poland where large assemblies were not allowed, was in effect a long-term programme of adult education in small discussion groups. So the book was limited in time, in space and in intent. Even then it was, according to Stefan Wilkanowicz, editor of *Znak*, the Kraków Catholic monthly, 'too difficult for the majority of people' (in *Nous Chrétiens de Pologne*, p. 100). So true was this that Halina Bortnowska, a Kraków theologian, was given the task of producing a more accessible version.

Nevertheless in Polish terms the publication of *Sources of Renewal* was an extremely important event. For it represented a commitment to the Council that was not universally found among Polish Bishops and was certainly not displayed by the Primate, Cardinal Stefan Wyszyński. For proof one has only to turn to the meeting between Pope Paul VI and thirty-eight Polish Bishops on 13 November 1965. The Pope was receiving national hierarchies in turn to bid them farewell as the Council drew to a close. He could hardly believe his ears when Cardinal Wyszyński addressed him as follows:

We are aware that it will be very difficult, but not impossible, to put the decisions of the Council into effect in our situation. Therefore we ask the Holy Father for one favour: complete trust in the episcopate and the Church of our country. Our request may appear very presumptuous, but it is difficult to judge our situation from afar. Everything that occurs in the life of our Church must be assessed from the standpoint of our experiences . . . If one thing is painful to us, it is above all the lack of understanding among our brothers in Christ. (Quoted in Hansjakob Stehle, *Eastern Politics of the Vatican, 1917–1979*, pp. 341–2)

Pope Paul coolly replied that no doubt the Council would be implemented 'energetically and willingly' in Poland. As he looked round the thirty-eight Bishops, it might have occurred to him that the young Archbishop of Kraków might fulfil the task that the Primate found so difficult. He was to make him a cardinal in 1967, welcomed his support for *Humanae Vitae* in 1968, and invited him to give a retreat to the Roman Curia in 1976. Clearly, Archbishop Wojtyla was the coming man. But on that November day in 1965 Paul VI gave orders that only his speech, and not that of Wyszyński, should appear in *L'Osservatore Romano*.

But why was Wyszyński so worried? He had been alarmed at the Council's lack of enthusiasm for popular piety, for the processions and pilgrimages which were such an important part of Polish piety. He was disconcerted by its understated mariology. He did not like liturgical change, believing that its effects would be unsettling, and he maintained that the new-fangled 'kiss of peace' would turn the church into a salon. As for ecumenism, it was irrelevant in Poland. Above all, the Council's eagerness to 'learn from the world' and its lack of any direct condemnation of communism would, he believed, sow confusion in his well-disciplined ranks. In short, from whatever angle you looked at it, the Council made things more difficult for the Polish Bishops. What the laity might or might not think was another matter.

No Polish Bishop, no Polish Cardinal even, publicly challenged the Cardinal Primate. His reputation as champion of the faith and the need for unity saw to that. But read in context, *Sources of Renewal* is an attempt by the Cardinal Archbishop of Kraków, twenty years junior to Wyszyński, delicately to suggest how and why the Council was relevant in Poland too. Wyszyński had said that it would be 'difficult, but not impossible' to perform this task. Wojtyla sets out to show positively how it is possible.

There was another consideration. He wanted to do justice to the historic event of the Council. He relished sharing in history in the making in this vast theological seminar which introduced him to a wider world of theological thinking. He found he could hold his own with no sense of inferiority. So *Sources of Renewal* was also the fulfilment of 'a debt to Vatican II'. He explains:

> The Council had a unique and unrepeatable meaning for all who took part in it, and most particularly for the bishops who were Fathers of the Council. These men took an active part for four years in the proceedings of the Council, drafting its documents, and at the same time deriving great *spiritual enrichment* from it. The experience of a world-wide community was to each of them a tremendous benefit of historic importance. The history of the Council, which will one day be written, was present in 1962–1965 as an extraordinary event in the minds of all the bishops concerned: it absorbed all their thoughts and stimulated their sense of responsibility, as an exceptional and deeply felt experience. (*Sources of Renewal*, p. 9)

This is a rather odd way to speak of the Council. It is made to sound wholly content-less – as though its most remarkable feature was that it actually happened. Again, it is presented as a private spiritual experience of *Bishops*, as though the Council had not aroused expectations in everyone.

Elsewhere, Wojtyla presents the 'event' of the Council in another light. He sees in it a confirmation of his own philosophical work:

> While writing this book [in the first, Polish version], the author attended the Second Vatican Council and his participation in the proceedings stimulated and inspired

his thinking about the person. It suffices to say that one of the chief documents of the Council, the pastoral constitution *On the Church in the Modern World*, not only brings to the forefront the person and his calling, but also asserts the belief in his transcendent nature. The constitution asserts: 'The role and competence of the Church being what it is, she must in no way be confused with the political community, nor bound to any political system. For she is at once the sign and safeguard of the transcendence of the human person.' (*The Acting Person*, D. Reidel, Dordrecht, Holland, 1979, pp. 302–3, footnote 9. The quotation from *Gaudium et Spes* comes from No. 76)

It is understandable that a philosopher, or at least a Catholic philosopher, should be delighted to note this harmony between his book and what the Council says. But on the other hand, belief in the transcendent nature of the human person is not exactly a novelty in Christian thinking, nor has it usually been limited to transcending 'political systems'. In any case, whatever the reason for calling the Council, it was not simply to make such a declaration on the human person.

A third feature of Cardinal Wojtyla's presentation of the Council is that it appears as a wholly tranquil and harmonious event: one would never guess from his account that there had been rows at the time and controversy subsequently. But this is a fiction. Halina Bortnowska noted this characteristic, and commented on it in her introduction to *L'Arricchimento della Fede*, the simplified version of *Sources of Renewal*:

Sources of Renewal was a first and provisional sketch. The author hides behind numerous quotations from the Council. Often he does not give his own thoughts, but rather suggests: read this text in the light of that other text. The Council texts and they alone occupy the stage, and *there is no appeal to post-conciliar or even conciliar discussions*. One has a feeling of great abstractness and remoteness from the world of people seeking some guidance for their lives. (*L'Arricchimento della Fede*, Vatican Press, 1981, p. 17. My italics)

Bortnowska does not attempt to explain this 'abstractness' from people and history. But part of the explanation must surely be that over the book loomed the shadow of Cardinal Wyszyński with his well-known views. The Council had presented to the world the spectacle of Bishops disagreeing with each other in public, with vigour and sometimes with passion. In the West these conflicts received wide publicity. In Poland they were, and were to remain, unreported. To admit that divisions could exist among Bishops posed a threat to the Polish Bishops who prized unity above all else. And the Communist Party was poised, ready to exploit differences between Bishops who were 'for' the Council and those benighted Bishops who were 'against' it.

Consequently Cardinal Wojtyla presented a bland and reassuring version of the Council which stresses continuity rather than a break with the past, perduring identity rather than novelty. His emphasis falls on 'the enrichment of faith' (and not for nothing did this become the title of the reworked version of his book). No one doubts that the Second Vatican Council was an intense spiritual experience for all those who took part in it. And no one doubts that it led to an 'enrichment of faith' for all those touched by its influence. No sane person would wish to argue in favour of the impoverishment of faith.

Yet these two principles – the spiritual experience and the enrichment of faith – clearly cannot exhaust the meaning of the Council. Was there nothing else of interest going on? Quite evidently, the way the Council was 'received' in Poland differed from the way it was 'received' in the West; and 'reception' has always been an important factor in the theological evaluation of Councils. In the case of Vatican II, the rule was that the reception of the Council depended on previous expectations. In Holland, for example, the Council was a heady experience of liberation; in France people were more inclined to believe that the rest of the Church had at last caught up with the best thinking of the French Church; the Archbishop of Dublin, Dr John McQuaid, assured the Irish on his return from the Council that 'it will make no difference in Ireland'. In Poland there had been little media coverage of the event – there was never paper available for the Catholic press – and there were few expectations of any kind. For the Council had been trying to answer questions – about ecumenism, the Church, the priesthood and religious life – which had *simply not been put* in Poland. It is always difficult to understand an answer when one has not asked the question. This explains the fundamental difference in the 'reception' (and consequently the perception) of the Council in Poland and in the West.

In the West the Council was evaluated above all for what was *new*. As John XXIII had said, its purpose was to bring about the *aggiornamento* of the Church, a word that in the United States was frequently translated as 'up-dating'. Paul VI replaced this by the more religious term 'renewal'. But however one looked at it, change of some kind was to be expected, not of course change in the substance of doctrine but change in the way it was expressed. Pope John said this explicitly, and this sentence was later embodied in *Gaudium et Spes*: 'The substance of the ancient deposit of faith is one thing, and the way in which it is presented is another' (Opening speech at the Council, 11 October 1962, in *The Documents of Vatican II*, Ed. Walter J. Abbott, SJ, Chapman, 1965, p. 715). This simple distinction liberated theologians in the West. In their commentaries on Vatican II the emphasis fell on the new openings which the Council provided.

But while theologians elsewhere were, as they used to say, 'exploiting the insights of Vatican II', Cardinal Wojtyla in *Sources of Renewal* was pursuing a very different path. His concern was with what the Council reaffirmed. Indeed his account makes it very difficult to imagine just why the Council was summoned in the first place, since it can hardly have been called simply in order to leave everything as it was. Yet this is what John Paul II sometimes appears to be saying. In his address to the United States Bishops, he said this about the purpose of the Council:

> With great wisdom, John XXIII convoked the Second Vatican Council. Reading the signs of the times, he knew that what was needed was a Council of a pastoral nature, a Council that would reflect the great pastoral love and care of Jesus Christ the Good Shepherd for his People.

So far this was common ground with all commentators. But then came the distorting qualification:

> But he knew that a pastoral Council, to be genuinely effective, would need a strong doctrinal basis. And for this reason, precisely because the word of God is the only basis for every pastoral initiative, John XXIII made the following statement on the opening day of the Council, 11 October 1962: 'The greatest concern of the ecumenical Council is this: that the sacred deposit of Christian doctrine should be more effectively guarded and taught.' This explains Pope John's inspiration; this was what the New Pentecost was to be; this was why the Bishops of the Church – in the greatest manifestation of collegiality in the history of the world – were called together, 'so that the sacred deposit of Christian doctrine should be more effectively guarded and taught'. (5 October 1979)

So the purpose of the Council was *defensive*. It was a matter of warding off errors, of *preserving* the deposit of faith.

But John XXIII said the exact opposite. In that famous opening address to the Council he said:

> Our duty is not only to guard this precious treasure, as if

we were concerned only with antiquity, but to dedicate ourselves with an earnest will and without fear to that work which our era demands of us. (*The Documents of Vatican II*, p. 715)

That is clearly envisaged as a new task, one that can only be performed by the men and women of this generation. As for defending the 'deposit of faith', Pope John explained that the purpose of the Council was not to restate the doctrine 'which has been repeatedly taught by the Fathers and by ancient and modern theologians, and which is presumed to be well-known and familiar to all'. He added a significant phrase which Cardinal Wojtyla either did not notice or has blotted out of his memory: 'For that [i.e. to restate familiar doctrine] a Council was not necessary' (ibid., p. 715). John Paul II attributes to the Council a defensive aim which John XXIII specifically repudiated.

This misunderstanding, based on misquotation, is absolutely fundamental. If one is not agreed on what the Council was for, it will be impossible to assess its significance, importance and achievements. This explains why in reading *Sources of Renewal* one has, again and again, a sense of opportunities being missed and nuances overlooked. I will give two examples.

Twenty pages are devoted to 'the ecumenical attitude' (*Sources of Renewal*, pp. 310–29). It is a perfectly fair account, at least in the material sense, of the conciliar decree *On Ecumenism*. But Cardinal Wojtyla has no significant comment to make on the passage which reminds theologians that 'there is an order or "hierarchy" of truths, since they vary in their relationship to the foundation of Christian faith' (No. 11). Yet this is arguably one of the most important statements of the Council. It permitted, indeed it encouraged, Catholic theologians to 'articulate' their faith and to make a distinction between the kernel of faith and its penumbra. It permitted Catholics to think and behave as Christians first. They were no longer obliged to define their identity in terms of fish on Fridays and a ban on artificial birth control.

Cardinal Wojtyla's comment on this key sentence is chillingly bleak:

> These words prescribe a methodology of ecumenical studies which is of great importance for ecumenical dialogue. It must not be forgotten that 'many Christians do not understand the Gospel in the same way as Catholics, and do not admit the same solutions for the more difficult problems of modern society'. (*Sources of Renewal*, p. 323. The quotation is from the decree *On Ecumenism* No. 23)

He means moral problems such as contraception, abortion, divorce. By laying the stress from the outset on possible dangers, Cardinal Wojtyla was going clean contrary to the method proposed by John XXIII and Paul VI. Both insisted that one should seek out 'what unites rather than what divides' and that there is a 'convergence towards Christ', to use one of Paul VI's favourite expressions. And this comment, in any case, has told Poles nothing about the true meaning of 'order or "hierarchy" of truths'.

A second example of the way a potentially arresting idea is reduced to banality is the treatment given to 'signs of the times'. As conceived by John XXIII, this was a way of saying that 'what was happening in the world', its trends and tendencies, could be a coded message from the Holy Spirit. This did not mean blessing every contemporary fad or fashion. But it did mean listening hard before attempting to 'discern' the presence of the Spirit.

Sources of Renewal gives a most cursory treatment of the 'signs of the times'. Its principal role, says Cardinal Wojtyla, is to 'bring into prominence the historical consciousness of the Church, for it expresses the fact that the Church's mission of salvation requires essentially to be rooted in time, which shapes its history' (ibid., p. 165). This glosses over the main question which is: what is to be done with this new-found 'historical consciousness'? It is inadequate to note its existence without giving examples of the difference it might make. Moreover, he does not answer the crucial question: on whom does the task of discernment of the signs of the times fall? *Gaudium et Spes* is clear on this point: the task devolves on the *whole* Church (No. 4), on 'the entire people of God' though especially on 'pastors and theologians' (No. 44).

In John Paul's mature thinking, on the other hand, the task of discerning the signs of the times is assigned exclusively to the *magisterium*, which means the teaching authority of the Church and, in current practice, the pope. This decisive repeal of the Council was accomplished on 7 October 1979, when John Paul addressed the nuns gathered in the shrine of the Immaculate Conception in Washington:

> As daughters of the Church . . . you are called to a generous and loving adherence to the authentic *magisterium* of the Church, which is a solid guarantee of all your apostolates and an indispensable condition for the proper interpretation of the 'signs of the times'. (7 October 1979)

At this point the 'signs of the times approach', potentially so enriching because it admits that 'what is happening' may be a theological source alongside scripture and tradition, is domesticated and emasculated. This has practical and theoretical consequences. If for example religious women have decided, for good reasons, that the traditional religious habit has become an obstacle to their mission, because it arouses the wrong, out-of-this-world expectations, then they should abandon it. John Paul has made it clear on countless occasions that he disapproves. They have read the 'signs of the times'; he has imposed an act of authority.

One way of discovering where John Paul stands on the Council is to consider what account he gives of the left/right, liberal/progressive conflict in the Church. All the words are imprecise and wrong, but we have no better ones. In his first encyclical, *Redemptor Hominis*, he observed that Catholics were arguing with each other more than they did before the Council. On the one hand we have a shadowy group whose 'growing criticism is due to various causes, and we are furthermore sure that it was not always without a sincere love for the Church' (No. 4). Who are these people? Against them are ranged a rival group of whom it is said: 'Some even express the opinion that these ecumenical efforts are harmful to the cause of the Gospel, are leading to further division within the Church, are causing confusion of ideas in questions of faith and morals, and are leading in fact to indifferentism' (No. 6). Two of the four points made here – confusion on faith and morals and the peril of indifferentism – had already been made by Cardinal Wojtyla in *Sources of Renewal*. So he is sympathetic to this cause. That is why his comment is of the mildest: 'It is perhaps a good thing that the spokesmen for these opinions should express their fears' (No. 6). There is a curious contrast between the indulgence accorded to these fretting, timorous conservatives and the doubts cast on the sincerity of the 'critics'. In case of conflict, one knows on which side John Paul would come down.

In France the two groups are known as 'progressives' and 'integrists'. Here is how the progressives are described in John Paul's address to the French Bishops:

> They impatiently want to adapt to the demands of the 'world' the content of faith, Christian ethics, the liturgy, Church structures. But they do not take sufficient account not only of the *sensus communis* of the faithful who are disconcerted by all this, but of the already defined essentials of faith . . . They are obsessed with 'getting ahead', but towards what sort of progress are they really aiming? (1 July 1980)

It is impossible to say, because this portrait of a crazy wrecker, hell-bent on the destruction of the Church, is so obviously a caricature. And the portrait is already more sinister than in *Redemptor Hominis* where doubts were cast on his sincerity. Now he appears as a worldling.

What, then, about the 'integrists', the other group who have got things wrong? This could just refer – we were in France – to Archbishop Marcel Lefebvre and his men, who had occupied a Parisian church and challenged Church and State to throw them out. The trouble with them is that

> they have hardened their arteries and locked themselves up in one period of Church history, one stage of theological formulation or liturgical expression which they turn into an absolute . . . being afraid of new questions, and without admitting that in the end the Spirit of God is at work in the Church, in her pastors united to the successor of Peter. (ibid.)

Of the two errors, that of the integrists looks more capable of resolution. Lefebvre is invited to accept, before he dies, that 'the Spirit of God is at work in the Church, in her pastors united to the successors of Peter'. That should not prove too difficult. But there is no such hope for the 'progressives'. That was in France in July 1980.

In Germany in November 1980 the contrast between the two groups became sharper and the caricature more evident. This could be because of the proven soundness of the German Bishops in matters of orthodoxy. The French were less reliable. Now the 'progressives' were those who had 'falsely concluded, from the impetus given by Vatican II, that the dialogue on which the Church has embarked is incompatible with the clear commitment of the *magisterium* and the norms of the Church' (Fulda, 17 November 1980). What is even more remarkable is the leniency now extended to the integrists. First, their very existence is explained by the excesses of the 'progressives'. Then sympathy is extended to them because 'they no longer feel at home in the Church'. And finally there is a practical, pastoral tip for dealing with such unfortunates:

> Here one must say to such people with great decisiveness, but at the same time with great prudence, that the Church of Vatican II, of Vatican I, of the Council of Trent and of all the earlier Councils of the Church, is one and the same Church. (17 November 1980)

So in the end the 'integrist', conservative or traditionalist Catholic is mollycoddled with the consoling suggestion that there was nothing really new about Vatican II. Naturally he will only find this comforting if he believes it to be true. He is likely to harbour serious doubts about this attempt to 'assimilate' Vatican II to Vatican I and all previous Councils. For he can always ask the simple and fundamental question: if nothing at all has changed in the Church, what was the point of Vatican II?

The caricature of the 'progressive' also reveals another weakness of John Paul's habitual analysis of the present state of the Church. He assumes that there are only two extreme positions that can be adopted and are worth discussing. But this is clearly false. The 'middle ground' is where most people are, and it would be worth discussing their aspirations and pastoral needs. But this does not happen. John Paul does not rule the Church, as Paul VI tried to, from the centre. He is consciously partisan on all inner-church controversies. Yet, as we saw at the start of this chapter, he claims to be committed to the Council. His commitment is, I believe, perfectly sincere because, in Polish terms, he was convinced that compared with Cardinal Wyszyński, he was definitely 'for the Council'. Translated from Kraków to Rome and entrusted with the solicitude of all the Churches, he persists in this conviction, even though he finds the need to reinterpret the Council in a conservative sense. This has been the cause of many misunderstandings.

6

The Populist Catechist

'Populism', as Leo Labedz has said, involves three elements: a direct appeal to the people above the heads of political parties or other intermediaries; a belief that the people are superior in virtue to the degenerate group that is leading them astray; and an identification of the 'will of the people' with morality and justice (*The Fontana Dictionary of Modern Thought*, Fontana and Collins, 1977, p. 487).

When due allowance has been made for obvious differences, this describes John Paul's pontifical style. He has appealed to the people directly in the great mass rallies that have marked his international journeys. He is the greatest crowd-puller in the world in the 1980s, far eclipsing pop groups and politicians. He stopped a homily at Galway racecourse to tell the youth of Ireland, 'I love you, I love you': they had never heard that from their parish priests. In the spring of 1981 Italy was debating whether to restrict or liberalize its abortion laws. Undeterred by the fact that the 'lay' parties were complaining about a 'foreigner interfering in the internal affairs of Italy', John Paul joined wholeheartedly in the Pro-Life campaign and set an example to the Italian Bishops and the Christian Democratic Party who were, he believed, shilly-shallying. The withdrawal of the title 'Catholic theologian' from Hans Küng was motivated by a desire to save the people from out-of-touch intellectuals. The faithful, said the declaration of the Congregation of the Doctrine of Faith, 'have a sacred right to receive the word of God uncontaminated, and so they expect that vigilant care should be exercised to keep the threat of error from them' (15 December 1979).

There is, of course, another dimension to be added. John Paul does not travel round the world merely to get people on his side. He has a message for them. He is a good popular communicator. He is essentially a catechist, and by catechist here one means not just someone who teaches children (though that is a permissible sense), but someone who can hand on the Christian faith and make it intelligible and attractive to our contemporaries. The 'catechist' is inevitably a 'missionary', and their common task is 'evangelization'. This had been the theme of the 1974 Synod. John Paul recalled this on the occasion of Mission Sunday 1981:

> It belongs to the Pope to urge the missionary vocation on all his brothers in Christ. As supreme pastor of a wholly missionary Church, he tries to follow the example of Christ, 'the first and greatest evangelizer', and to place himself under the guidance of the Holy Spirit. (Published 11 August 1981. Mission Sunday was 11 October 1981)

And this was the primary reason for his apostolic and pastoral journeys round the world. 'I wanted to be,' he concluded, 'a kind of itinerant catechist.'

The good catechist likes to start from where people actually are, rather than from where they ought to be. This principle was derived from John Paul's experience in Poland where almost anything – historical memories, wall-paintings, the turn of the seasons, quotations from Polish authors – could be used as a starting point. A particularly revealing passage in his address to young people in Warsaw puts this in a poignant way:

> My fellow countrymen, I desire that my pilgrimage through this Polish land, in communion with all of you, should become a living catechesis, the integration of that catechesis which entire generations of our forebears have inscribed in our history. May this be the catechesis of all

the history of the Church, and at the same time the catechesis of our age.

The fundamental task of the Church is catechesis. In this way an ever more conscious faith is gradually introduced into the life of each generation, through the common efforts of the family, the parish, priests and pastors of souls, men and women catechists, the community, mass media and traditions. In fact the walls of the belltowers of our churches, the crucifixes at the crossroads, the sacred paintings on the walls of houses – all these, in some sense, are part of catechesis. (3 June 1979)

These public symbols of faith gain in importance the more they become rare or tend to vanish: this process had been taking place, systematically, in Poland and that is why one of the first things Solidarity did was to restore them – the huge cross erected outside the shipyard at Gdansk is only one example. But previously 'secularization' had been enforced. This explains why Cardinal Wojtyla was unwilling to give up voluntarily any public religious symbols such as the wearing of the religious habit: there was no point in doing the devil's work for him. Though this involves a 'defensive' view of faith as something to be preserved in spite of immense difficulties, it also has a positive aspect. John Paul said that the aim of catechesis was to produce an 'ever more conscious faith'. One may begin with popular religion but not end there. Faith has to be personally appropriated, internalized, otherwise it remains conventional folklore.

The catechetical principle of using whatever comes to hand means logically that each of John Paul's journeys has a different character. No country is a completely blank slate, though in Africa he did have some difficulty in discovering a 'tradition'. Each country has its history, its problems, its worries: with these the catechist must grapple. And in John Paul's mind, each country has its *shrines*. When he looks at the map of any given country, he sees more than the mountains and railways and airports and big cities. He also

sees the pilgrimage centres and the power-houses of prayer.
Pride of place in his map of Italy goes to the Holy House of
Loreto, to Assisi, because of its links with St Francis, and to
Monte Cassino because of St Benedict and the Polish war
cemetery. In France for a short stay, he insisted on going to
Lisieux, where are the remains of St Theresa of Lisieux, 'the
Little Flower'; and only the bullets of Mehemet Ali Agca
stopped him from going to Lourdes a year later. In Germany
he sought out the tomb of St Boniface, the Devon man who
evangelized the place, and the less well known Marian shrine
at Altötting. But it has to be confessed that none of these
shrines plays the same part in national life and religious
feeling that Czestochowa plays in Poland. In the United
States there is nowhere to go on pilgrimage; and the attempt
to build a mock-Czestochowa at Doylestown, Pennsylvania,
foundered on the rocks of a financial scandal. Yet John Paul
believes very strongly that pilgrimages have a vitally
important part to play in the religious revival he can see
coming.

On 17 October 1980 he addressed a body called the
Diocesan Association of Pilgrimages which had just finished
its annual conference at Lourdes. No doubt they got a cut-
price trip to Rome. Their problem is that they risk becoming
little more than glorified tour operators and travel agents,
differing only in the goal or object of the journeys they
organize. John Paul exhorted them to 'get beyond questions
of organization, transport, costs, accommodation, which of
course have their importance, and to rack your brains so as
to set the minds and hearts of your pilgrims on the path of
conversion'. Then came the crucial passage:

> Love passionately this service you render to the Church.
> Though perhaps eclipsed in the recent past, pilgrimages
> are now developing once more in all parts of the world,
> and they are appreciated more than ever . . .
>
> Dear friends, *you have in your hands the key to the
> religious future of the age*. Christian pilgrimages, re-

discovered and relived in all their dimensions and demands, may well correspond to a more or less conscious need of contemporary man who is dissatisfied with his materialistic environment. Religious gatherings, spurned by some, could enable them to avoid the adventure of belonging to groups which seek in ambivalent sources a certain human and religious warmth. (17 October 1980)

This last sentence is particularly difficult to construe. It contrasts mass gatherings with small groups or *communautés de base*. 'Adventurism' is the Marxist term for those who risk splitting the party. It is hard to know why small meetings should be more ambivalent than mass gatherings. The Pope concluded:

The time has come to give to the pastoral work of pilgrimages at least as much importance as that given to the formation of élites. It is desirable to encourage both, without opposing them, in a complementary and dynamic manner. (ibid.)

This is the most important – and surprising – statement about pastoral priorities so far in the pontificate.

In another address – this time to Rectors of French shrines – John Paul repeated all this and added some further considerations. Pilgrimages were a constant feature of the history of religions generally. They are 'deeply rooted in the popular mind and correspond to a desire to go to the place where the divine was manifested'. It is again asserted that pilgrimages are on the up and up (*en pleine remontée*). They are a powerful means of evangelization and unbelievers are attracted to them because 'they feel the asphyxia of a society enclosed within itself and sometimes in despair'. Pilgrimage centres should have a complete pastoral programme and organize doctrinal and spiritual lectures. This is needed because 'many important teachings of the *magisterium* are practically ignored or only confusedly grasped' (22 January 1981).

There can be no doubt that John Paul is here describing, in a somewhat idealized way, what actually happens on a Polish pilgrimage, especially to Czestochowa. It is a long and tough hike, often lasting over a week. There is prayer and religious discussion along the route. There is the solidarity of shared fatigue and blisters. And at the end, there is the magical vision of Jasna Gora (the 'Bright Mountain') and Mass at the shrine of the Black Madonna. It is easy in these circumstances to pass from this particular pilgrimage to the idea that all of life is a pilgrimage, a quest and that we are all *in via*.

But not all pilgrimages are like this. Loreto, for example, is a hilltop town near Ancona on the Adriatic, where a small building said to have been the house of the Holy Family at Nazareth was allegedly transported by celestial means. That was on a May day in 1291. Peter Nichols concedes that the number of pilgrims to places like Loreto is growing, but is less convinced that there are no undesirable side effects:

Loreto may strain anyone's sense of credulity but its custodians maintain that there is a growing tendency among ordinary people to give immediate credence to claims of miracles or divine visitations. A woman living near Loreto spent her time writing down messages and warnings and instructions which came, she said, directly from Jesus. He had asked her to build him a church on a hill quite close to the massive shrine of Loreto but to make it even larger than St Peter's in Rome. (*The Pope's Divisions*, Faber and Faber, 1981, p. 189)

John Paul visited Loreto in September 1979. He had nothing to say about its 'ambivalence'.

One feature of John Paul's vocabulary is that he describes each journey he makes as a 'pilgrimage'. Every time he gets out of a plane and kisses the ground, he announces that he has arrived on a 'pilgrimage'. He once described a meeting with a group of Bishops as 'a pilgrimage to the heart of the Church'. A classic use of the concept came at the opening of his address to the German Evangelical Church leaders:

> I recall that in 1510–11 Martin Luther went to Rome as a pilgrim to the tomb of the apostles, and also to find an answer to some questions. Today I come to you, to the spiritual heirs of Martin Luther; I come as a pilgrim to make this meeting in a changed world a sign of union in the central mystery of our faith. (Mainz, 17 November 1980)

An Evangelical might well have been distracted by wondering whether John Paul was a 'pilgrim' in the same sense as Luther, and what answer Luther got to his questions. A word that can be used so universally and indiscriminately has very little stuffing left in it. But what the word does is to 'sacralize' the Pope and his journeys. To call him 'the pilgrim pope' is a reminder of his religious mission; to call him 'the globe-trotting pope' would be to try to cut him down to secular size.

So John Paul has exhorted the Church to go on pilgrimages; and presented his own journeys as pilgrimages. Here we see two facets of his populism. For his journeys round the world have – with the exception of the visits to Turkey in November 1978 and Japan in February 1981 – been popular triumphs. No one has been disappointed – or if they have, they kept quiet about it. After a time, national competitiveness adds to the excitement. The youth of America did not wish to appear less enthusiastic than the youth of Ireland, and the youth of France did not wish to appear less enthusiastic than the youth of America. Television creates this kind of emulation. In Africa people were enthusiastic simply because the Pope had come to see them: the King of the Ashanti does not get many visitors in Kumasi, Ghana; the Moslems of Ouagadougou, capital of

Upper Volta, are a particularly hospitable lot. After the assassination attempt, a new motive for acclaiming the Pope began to exist: he is the survivor, and everyone wants to see how well he really is. In short, any 'pilgrim pope' is likely to get a good reception from large crowds in most places.

But it is undeniable that the personal charism of John Paul has helped to make these occasions unforgettable for those who were there. A charism cannot be analysed. But a style can. What I want to attempt in the rest of this chapter is an analysis of the *rhetoric* of John Paul. The word carries with it no pejorative note. It refers neutrally to how he speaks in public. This literary analysis will of necessity be incomplete and rather unsatisfactory, since one is dealing in another language with texts that have been *thought out* in Polish first. They have then been translated by bureaucrats. Few poets could survive such a linguistic mauling. Yet it is surprising how much of John Paul's personal style comes through. And it is essentially a populist style, designed for maximum impact on big assemblies. This could be seen in his sermons and addresses in Brazil in July 1980.

There were exuberant crowds everywhere. It was fiesta time. In Fortaleza he inaugurated the Brazilian National Eucharistic Congress. Its theme was 'Where are you going?', which may seem rather curious but was in fact an invitation to consider some of the practical problems of Brazil: one of them is 'inner emigration' which has all but destroyed the original Indian population, and has sent many people from the North to the South in the somewhat vain and desperate hope of finding work. The homily skilfully interwove this human experience and its theological interpretation, without any sense of strain. The problems of inner emigration were faced squarely; but they were at the same time counter-pointed with the words of Peter in John's Gospel: 'To whom shall we go, Lord? Your words are the words of eternal life' (John 6:68). In this way the 'emigrant' or the 'internal immigrant' became the type of the human pilgrimage generally, 'wandering along the streets of the world, journeying in the shadow of the provisional, in search of the true peace and joy for which our hearts are hungry' (9 July 1980). The 'itinerant catechist' had found the right wavelength.

Two days earlier, at Porto Alegre, John Paul had spoken on the theory of catechesis. 'Popular religiosity' used to be enough: now this is no longer so because of 'the spread of culture, a growth in the spirit of criticism, and the mass media'. Yet Christianity is not just a *doctrine* to be contemplated but a *message* to be acted upon. It follows that the catechist is not just 'propounding ideas so much as evoking a response'. Moreover, his message is 'not addressed to some imaginary, abstract hearers, but to particular people living at a particular time, with their own hopes and dramas'. The union of the message and doctrine was brilliantly expressed in a single sentence: 'For a child there is no difference between his *mother praying* and *prayer*' (Porto Alegre, 5 July 1980). However, he also added that the appropriate setting for catechesis was the *parish*. This may sound a banality, until one remembers that the entire pastoral policy of the Brazilian Bishops is founded on 'basic communities', small groups living and applying the Gospel on the local community level. In their context the parish is often a larger and more abstract unity.

But not all John Paul's utterances in Brazil were in this 'catechetical' style. There was another kind of address, longer, more ornate, more academic, in which he sketched out mini-treatises on urgent social problems. Long before the encyclical *Laborem exercens* was published, its basic ideas had been tried out before a variety of audiences. When John Paul adopts this tone, his style changes: it becomes grave, knowing and expository. The old philosophy professor takes over. The main feature of this style is its clarity. Its yes is a yes and its no is a no. Doubt or hesitancy do not enter in. He lectures the 'world'. In El Salvador (the Brazilian city, not the Central American country), addressing 'the builders of a pluralist society', a Catholic movement which had been inspired by Puebla and which brought together trades unionists, planners, teachers, journalists, scientists, he said: 'The Church, founded by Christ, shows contemporary man the way he must go to build up the earthly city which, despite its imperfections, foreshadows the heavenly city' (7 July 1980). Were the term not already pre-empted, it would be appropriate to call this style 'magisterial'.

No one who speaks as much as John Paul can get away without using certain stylistic devices, which are all part of the classical repertoire. Here are some examples. He makes frequent use of what used to be called the *captatio benevolentiae*, which means flattering people and getting them on your side. In Brazil it often took the form: 'I could not possibly come to Brazil without having a meeting with the people of X or Y.' The people of X and Y then cheer wildly, imagining that a remarkable favour has been bestowed on them. A variant of this device is to say: 'I would like to greet you all personally/to enter every Brazilian home/to sit down for a meal with every family/to embrace every leper – but unfortunately, as you well realize, this is impossible.'

Another effective device is the evocation of a personal experience. Addressing young people in Belo Horizonte he declared that in his youth he had shared their desire to sweep away unjust social structures. Like them, he found it impossible to be happy while vast numbers of his fellow citizens were in misery. 'As a young man,' he said, 'I expressed these ideas in poetry and literature.' Then came the war. His ideals were mocked and trampled upon. They seemed to have been swept away in the whirlwind of war. 'One day,' concluded John Paul, 'I brought these ideals to Christ, and understood that he alone could reveal their true context and value' (1 July 1980). Another wartime memory was evoked in Fortaleza:

During the harsh and terrible war in Poland I saw young

people leave without hope of returning, parents snatched from their homes without knowing whether they would ever see their loved ones again. At the moment of parting there would be a gesture, or a photograph or some object would pass from hand to hand in order to prolong presence even in absence. (Fortaleza, 9 July 1980)

The purpose of this passage was not directly autobiographical: it was to contrast human love with divine love, which in the Eucharist is a permanent and effective symbol of 'presence in absence'. But it gains in effectiveness thanks to its autobiographical content. This is a man speaking, not a disembodied handbook. But wartime Poland must seem remote from contemporary Brazil.

The apostrophe, frequently used by John Paul, tends to nonplus his hearers. It is usually reserved for the conclusion of a homily. A good example occurred at Belen, where he suddenly turned towards the statue of Our Lady and began to address that which it represents: 'Mary, you are the Second Eve . . .' Six other invocations followed. There was a transition from preaching to praying (Belen, 8 July 1980).

Lastly, John Paul uses a device which belongs as much to psychology as to rhetoric. It consists in a quotation from the very person or persons whom he is addressing. It is most commonly used with Bishops (so for example the American Bishops in Chicago, 5 October 1979), who are gratified at hearing their own words and yet also feel, in some cases, that they are hoist with their own petard. They did indeed say x, but they didn't mean it in quite that way. In Brazil John Paul played the same trick on President João Figueiredo. If reforms are to be realized, he told the President, then mentalities have to be changed, 'always enlightened by "the certainty that man is at the centre of our concerns and responsibilities", as you wrote to me recently' (30 June 1980). It was a shrewd move. The President could hardly object to having his own words quoted back at him, even though, considering his autocratic ways, they may be no more than a hollow flourish. But he said it, and should be made to stick to it.

At Belen in Brazil, John Paul was preaching at a Marian shrine. His text was 'Henceforward all generations will call me blessed' (Luke 1:48). There he summed up his view on 'popular religiosity':

> Popular religiosity, normally bound up with devotion to Our Lady, certainly needs enlightening, guiding and purifying. But if it really is — as my predecessor Paul VI called it — 'the devotion of the poor and the simple', then it contains a real 'thirst for God'. Anyway, it does not have to be a vague feeling or an inferior manifestation of the religious spirit. It can contain, very often, a deep sense of God and his attributes, a sense of paternity, providence, loving presence, and mercy. (Belen, 8 July 1980)

Most of the difficulties in understanding John Paul II fade away once one has grasped that popular religion is what counts for him. The Council and the post-conciliar period underestimated it. It is now making a come-back.

7

The Message and the Cribs of Kraków

We saw in the last chapter that John Paul II has a populist style, a traditional rhetoric, and that he wants to revive and stimulate 'popular religion' throughout the Church. The borderline between form and content is always difficult to determine; and in talking about 'style' one already strays over into the realm of *what* is being said. Here I want to set down as simply as possible what is, for John Paul, the gist of the Christian message. What has he got to say?

Such is the flood of words in this pontificate that we are in danger of losing our grip on essentials and being drowned in the spate. An introduction should be able to put together an emergency-kit for survival after the flood has passed over. So I take as my starting point the simplest possible statement. One Sunday morning in Lent 1981, John Paul appeared as usual at the fourth-floor window of the Apostolic Palace and said:

'Behold, I stand at the door and knock' [Revelation 3:20]. These words of the Apocalypse recur in the liturgy of Lent and bring before our eyes the image of Christ who, especially at this time of year, *knocks at the hearts and consciences of human persons*.

He knocks so that they may be opened to him, because he wants them to begin a conversation with him, that 'dialogue of salvation' of which Paul VI spoke in his first encyclical. Yes, Christ *wants to speak* with every man of our time, just as he spoke with Nicodemus, the Samaritan woman, the young man with many possessions and Mary

Magdalen. Christ is *the most wonderful interlocutor*, who deals with the deepest and most difficult problems, always in the fullness of truth and with total love for man.

Yes, Christ wants to speak with every man. To speak with him incessantly. To speak with families, different social groups, with entire nations. To speak constantly with the whole of humanity: to speak of fundamental problems, of *the most important problems* on which the dignity of man on earth and his eternal salvation depend.

Behold, he stands at the door and knocks!

Christ, who stands at the door of human consciences and knocks, speaks through the mediation of those who are the successors of the apostles and the servants of the salvation of every man. (22 March 1981)

Except for the final sentence, which seems to limit unduly the possibilities of Christ's action, there is little here that any Christian preacher would want to quarrel with. I want to use this passage to bring out the personal accent in which John Paul couches the age-old Christian message.

His starting point is always Christ, the alpha and the omega, the hinge of history, the ultimate point of reference. He has sometimes quoted Charles Péguy, the French poet: 'The incarnation is the most interesting story ever told.' It is 'interesting' not because it satisfies curiosity but because it gives meaning to the lives of individuals and to human history. John Paul has a very 'high' christology. He sees Christ in terms of John's Gospel as 'the Word of God' with us, the *logos* by whom the world is ordered, very God translated into human language and made accessible ('Who sees me, Philip, sees the Father' – John 14:9). And this 'image' of Christ is filled out by the Pauline concept of him as 'Second Adam', the one in whom the human race, previously scattered and bewildered, is enabled to pick itself up and set off along the God-intended path of unity and grace. Since Mary, in John's Gospel, stands at the foot of the cross of Jesus, she is associated with his passion and becomes the

'Second Eve' alongside the Second Adam. The apostle John is a representative figure, so that when Jesus says to Mary, 'Woman, behold thy son', this maternity extends to all the disciples of Jesus. John Paul's mariology, which both sustains and is sustained by his christology, takes its origin here.

Rudolf Bultmann taught several generations of theologians to distinguish between 'the Jesus of history' (who was inaccessible) and 'the Christ of faith' (who could be reached through the early Christian communities and thus solve the existential problems of Modern Man). John Paul rejects this distinction utterly, because he believes that it is ruinous of faith (and so it is if the *distinction* is turned into a *separation*). The result, however, is that he tends to read the Synoptic Gospels (Matthew, Mark and Luke) in the light of the fully developed christology found in John and Paul. This is the basis for the misunderstanding with Edward Schillebeeckx, who has a keener historical sense, is concerned not just with the end-result of christology but with its genesis, and has tried to restate the 'forgotten truths' contained in the Synoptics. The difference here is a matter of emphasis. The irony is that Schillebeeckx wrote his books partly as an antidote to Bultmann.

John Paul's Christ, then, stands outside – as in Holman Hunt's celebrated painting of Christ as the Light of the World – and knocks at the door of human hearts. His message is not an authoritative monologue nor a harangue, but an invitation to a conversation. It is intended to evoke a response (called 'faith'), to bring about change (known as 'conversion' or *metanoia*) and to inaugurate a dialogue (which is prayer). The response, the change and the dialogue touch the deepest levels of the human personality. The message cannot be allowed to loll inertly on the surface of the mind. It requires an answer that is responsible, lucid, self-committing and mature – that is, not just the fulfilment of infantile needs for a father or a mother figure. This is the 'more conscious faith' we saw in the last chapter.

Moreover, Christ is *our contemporary*. We do not get in touch with him merely through the powers of imagination or memory. He is present in the living community of the Church, in its worship, and in the continuous stream of tradition, which is not a dead hand weighing down from the past but the *memoria* and conscience of the Church. There is a sense in which, to borrow Bossuet's phrase, the Church is 'the Incarnation continued'. But right at the end of this little homily, John Paul slipped in his ecumenically disconcerting phrase about Christ speaking 'through the mediation of the successors of the apostles'. Protestants traditionally stress fidelity to the *teaching* of the apostles rather than to their *successors*. But many would be able to accept that Christ 'speaks through the successors of the apostles'. But then the question arises: is this the only way in which he speaks? What about the innumerable disguises Christ can wear in the oppressed and the poor? What about the mother teaching her child to pray, the abandoned wife reading the gospels, the nurse tending the impossible patient? No doubt John Paul would not object to any of this – and one cannot say everything every time. But once again there is a difference of emphasis that could have wider consequences.

But the corner-stone of John Paul's christology is this: Christ, the Word of God, the Second Adam, our contemporary and brother, speaks to us not only of the wonderful works of God, the *magnalia Dei*, but of our own situations, individual and collective. To judge by the number of times he uses it, his favourite quotation from *Gaudium et Spes* is concerned with Christ as Second Adam: 'Christ, the final Adam, by the revelation of the mystery of the Father and his love, *fully reveals man to man himself*, and makes his supreme calling clear' (No. 22). The interest of this text is that it implies that Christian revelation is as much about man as it is about God. We are accustomed to think and speak as though all the mystery were on the side of God and man were completely transparent to himself. But this is not really so: he is a confused bundle of conflicting impulses and aspirations.

In the Second Adam he discovers his 'supreme calling', his vocation, a sense of direction and focus. This is the thinking behind John Paul's 'appeal to the nations' that was one of the most eloquent parts of the homily at the inauguration Mass:

> Open wide the doors to Christ. To his saving power open the boundaries of states, economic and political systems, the vast fields of culture, civilization and development. Do not be afraid. Christ 'knows what is in man'. He alone knows it. (22 October 1978)

Everything else he has said about human rights, the world of work, culture and peace, can be seen as an expansion of this statement. There is nowhere where Christ is not at home, nowhere where his message is irrelevant.

In the last chapter I quoted a passage in which John Paul said that in Poland, so many things speak of Christ, 'the walls of the belltowers of our churches, the crucifixes at the crossroads, the sacred paintings on the walls of houses – all these, in some sense, are part of catechesis' (3 June 1979, supra, p. 70). To this list should be added the characteristic cribs of Kraków. A brief consideration of them will show the depth of popular piety, confirm the dominance of a 'high' christology, and have a special poignancy after the events of Christmas 1981.

The cribs of Kraków (*szopka*) are quite unlike Italian cribs and make a different point. The idea of making cribs goes back to St Francis of Assisi. He wanted to bring out the ordinariness of this extraordinary event: God becoming man. It was also a form of prayer. You kneel at the crib, imagine yourself there, and pray. Though the baroque tradition brought endless complications to this simple theme, the Italian crib continued to say something about the humanity of Jesus and the homeliness of his coming among us.

The Kraków cribs are not ordinary at all. They are

twinkling faery palaces. They are ablaze with colour and gold and silver. You have to look hard to find the stable. It is there, of course, but enshrined (in the literal sense of 'turned into a shrine') in the magnificent façade which, as one comes closer, is seen to be modelled on one of the many churches of Kraków. Though it occupies the central place, the stable is almost overwhelmed by the splendour which surrounds it. But since the child in the stable is the *raison d'être* of the whole work, the dazzling setting becomes a celebration of the kingship of Christ. Though he does not at this moment look like a king, in fact he eclipses the glory of all earthly kings. In a Christmas sermon in Wawel Cathedral, Kraków, Cardinal Wojtyla pointed out that it was a *royal* cathedral (and indeed the last kings of Poland lie buried in its crypt). So he had an easy transition to the theme of Christ as the king of kings.

The christology of the Kraków cribs is based on the prologue to John's Gospel: 'In the beginning was the Word, and the Word was with God, and the Word was God ... And the Word was made flesh and dwelt amongst us' (John 1:1, 14). Italian cribs – and most of the world has followed this lead – are based on Luke's Gospel: 'Mary wrapped him round and laid him in the manger, because there was no room at the inn' (2:7). The shepherds arrive. The artists assume the presence of animals. It is a touching story of refugee homelessness. But where Italian cribs try to humanize the event, the cribs of Kraków sacralize it. Italian cribs bring the reality of the Incarnation home. Kraków cribs fill us with wonder and awe at the birth of the new and transcendent king. Their fantastic turrets are like a dream which contrasts with the drabness of everyday life. There is usually a patriotic note as well: a Polish eagle surmounts the whole, and the red and white flag of Poland flutters from the topmost spires, while the blue and white flag of Kraków is found at a lower level.

Sometimes the crib-makers comment on what is happening by simple juxtaposition. The ground floor is often occupied by a dramatic scene. This is not so surprising since the cribs were originally designed as puppet theatres. A favourite scene shows Herod, seated on a throne, while around him courtiers posture and make speeches. At least it looks like Herod: but it could be General Wojciech Jaruzelski. The point is the same in any case: do not be misled by appearances. The king down below in ermine and gold may seem to be more powerful and prestigious. But on the floor above, Jesus, the real king, is born.

There is a perfect match between the implied theology of the Kraków cribs, and the christology of John Paul. In the last Christmas sermon he gave in Kraków, in 1977, he made clear the link between his christological statement and the political message to be drawn from it:

> The rights of man correspond to humanity, to that dignity which God, by becoming man, has confirmed. It is wrong to limit these rights in any way. You cannot say: you have rights, but only because you belong to this nation, this race, this social class, this party. The rights of man belong to human nature itself, and that is what God says to us in the mystery of Christmas, since he became man so that each of us could become a son of God. (K. Wojtyla, *Discorsi al Populo di Dio, 1976–1978*, Centro Studi Europa Orientale, Bologna, 1978, p. 64)

With that simple statement, volumes of Marxist theorizing were consigned to the dustbin.

The onion domes of many Kraków cribs remind us that we are halfway across Europe. The cribs are not *icons* in the literal and Orthodox sense. But they resemble icons in their stylized attitudes, their rootedness in folk art, and the emphasis on the glory and splendour that surrounds the new-born king. They strongly suggest that the key to the universe is already there and is available on the first floor.

8

Intellectuals to the Rescue

Very few Britons own up to being 'intellectuals'. The word survives as a term of abuse. But in the culture from which John Paul II emerges, matters are very different. Raymond Williams tells us that 'intellectual' (with its plural, *intelligentsia*) emerged in the Russia of the 1860s where it designated that section of the university-educated youth who engaged in 'critical thinking' or were 'nihilist'. In France, it was sometimes used, in praise or blame, for those who sprang to the defence of Captain Alfred Dreyfus. For Marx, intellectuals were those members of the bourgeoisie 'who attached themselves to the working-class with the function of shaping their ideas', as Williams charmingly puts it (*The Fontana Dictionary of Modern Thought*, p. 324). But not all intellectuals have been on the left. In Poland those Catholics who fitted the general description belonged to bodies called 'Clubs of Catholic Intellectuals'. So John Paul is surprised and sceptical when other countries are chary about producing their intellectuals. For all his populism, he needs to have them on his side.

When his journey to France was already arranged for June 1980, he looked at the programme and exclaimed, 'What, no meeting with intellectuals? Everywhere I go I meet intellectuals.' It is not difficult to find intellectuals in Paris, so the Papal Nuncio hastily arranged a breakfast for them at his residence, 10 avenue Wilson. John Paul started the ball rolling with the question: 'What do you think of the way the world is going?' One hour later the breakfast was over, and they had still not managed to complete their first *tour de table*. Non-invited intellectuals later complained that the twenty or so favoured guests were 'somewhat of the right'.

They order these things better in Germany. On Saturday, 15 November 1980, over four thousand people were crammed into Cologne Cathedral. Here the labels changed somewhat. They were not described as 'intellectuals' but as 'men of science and learning', in short *Wissenschaftler*. That four thousand such people should exist in West Germany I would not presume to doubt; that they should all have been gathered in Cologne Cathedral on a snowy Saturday afternoon seems a little improbable; in fact a number of schoolboys and students were drafted to make up the numbers.

The message John Paul had for the German 'men of science and learning' was intriguing. The occasion for the visit to West Germany, and the pretext for the meeting with the *Wissenschaftler*, was that this very 15 November 1980 was the seven hundredth anniversary of the death, in Cologne, of St Albert the Great, Dominican and teacher of St Thomas Aquinas. Now although the University of Cologne bears his name (the Albertinum), it must be confessed that Albert is not exactly a live intellectual force in Germany today, and that though his courage and ability to cover immense distances on foot are widely admired, few could quote a single memorable sentence from his works. Moreover, a lady theologian had suggested that he was anti-feminist, believing that a girl was the result of an unsuccessful attempt to produce a boy – the operation being impeded by the south wind blowing in from Africa. She also alleged that he was anti-Semitic. This was not a promising background for a consideration of the relevance of Albert the Great today.

John Paul solved the problem by neat footwork. 'The content of Albert's work,' he roundly confessed, 'is often time-bound, but his method of uniting faith and reason has exemplary value for us today.' Thus Albert became a symbolic figure. He expresses the need not only for a reconciliation between science and faith but for a *positive partnership* between science and faith. John Paul's vision is certainly bold. He was not just saying that 'there can be no conflict between science and faith, provided science follows its own methods', though he did of course say that. More fundamentally he claimed that new questions requiring new answers were emerging, and that these could lead the Church and science into a new stage of co-operation.

Three examples. The whole ecological movement can be seen as setting a question mark against the notion of 'progress' which was so naïvely accepted in the last century. 'Progress' is dethroned if its side effects or unintended consequences can prove to be so catastrophic. Next, the 'human sciences' (psychology, sociology) have sometimes abandoned a concern for 'meaning' and 'truth', so that the very concept of reason itself is put in jeopardy (John Paul was probably thinking of Michel Foucault). Various ideologies have rushed in to fill the 'meaning-vacuum', but now they are universally discredited. This 'crisis of ideologies' gives the Church its chance.

John Paul is an apologist: he wants to defend Christianity as a rational faith that can 'give an account of the hope that is in it'. He told the four thousand German *Wissenschaftler* that in the eighteenth century, the enemies of the Church used to attack its teaching with the slogan, 'Reason, Freedom, Progress'. But now it is the Church that has become the champion of these ideas. Christians defend Reason – against various irrationalist philosophies. They defend Freedom – against the tyrannies based on ideological systems. And they defend Progress – against the temptation to pessimism to which so many are prone. 'A new alliance between faith and science is called for,' cried John Paul, 'and a new humanism for the third millennium.' This grandiose vision is the scientific underpinning of the project for the spiritual reunification of Europe which provides the impetus for this pontificate.

So what John Paul expects from the 'men of science and learning' is perfectly clear: they are to contribute to the synthesis of science and faith. He has completely shaken up the hitherto slumbering Pontifical Academy of Sciences. His first move was to 'rehabilitate' Galileo, who since Beyle's *Dictionnaire* at the end of the seventeenth century had been used by rationalists as the symbol of Roman Catholic obscurantism. Then, with that problem out of the way, in 1981 he set the members of the Pontifical Academy of Sciences to work: they went to five world leaders to acquaint them with the devastating effects of nuclear weapons. This corresponds very much to John Paul's constant insistence on the *moral* role of scientists. At Hiroshima in February 1981, his message was again addressed to scientists all the world over. Scientists were responsible for making these weapons; they should therefore be the first in urging that they should be dismantled (25 February 1981).

But not all intellectuals are scientists. John Paul requires literary intellectuals as well. The task they are assigned is that of rethinking, and eventually rewriting, the intellectual history of Europe. The reason this is necessary is because he believes that somewhere along the road – most probably at the Renaissance – Europe took a wrong turning, the lamentable effects of which can still be seen today. This means, in effect, a rejection of the mainstream of the European tradition. That John Paul holds such views was made clear in his address to a Congress on 'Atheism and Evangelization':

Modern man, since the Renaissance, in a tremendous challenge [*un gigantesque défi*], rose up against the mystery of salvation, and began to refuse God in the name of the dignity of man. At first limited to a small group, the intelligentsia that considered itself an élite, atheism today has become a mass phenomenon which assails the Churches. What is more, atheism infiltrates into the hearts of believers themselves, including those who call on the name of Jesus Christ, and brings about a secret and ruinous complicity in the undermining of faith in God –

and does so in the name of the autonomy and dignity of man. (10 October 1980)

Mass atheism, then, assails the Church from all sides, and has even penetrated within the citadel itself. That sounds a most sinister suggestion. What will happen to such traitors when they are unmasked?

In his sketch of the Church imperilled by atheism, John Paul makes no distinction between what he calls 'the socialist countries and the capitalist countries', even though there is an obvious difference between the systematically inculcated atheism of, say, the Soviet Union, and the more haphazard process of 'secularization' that has taken place in the West. But John Paul not only does not make such a distinction: he rejects it. When he went to Turin, headquarters of the Fiat car industry, now in recession, he denounced impartially the two intellectual forces which have shaped the modern world, liberalism and Marxism:

> There is on the one hand the rationalist, scientistic, Enlightenment approach of the so-called secular 'liberalism' of Western nations, which carries with it the radical denial of Christianity; and on the other hand the ideology and praxis of atheistic 'Marxism' whose materialistic principles are taken to their most extreme consequences in various forms of contemporary terrorism. (13 April 1980)

That, at least, was the version of the speech contained in the press hand-outs. In actual delivery, the link between Marxism and terrorism was toned down – no doubt because it was pointed out to him that it was grossly unfair, since Italian communists have been as opposed to terrorism as the Christian Democrats. But the result was that the condemnation of 'so-called secular "liberalism"' seemed harsher and stronger than the predictable attack on Marxism.

This is a view of Western European intellectual history

which leaves no room for dialogue. There is simply nothing to be learned from the two main currents of the European tradition, since they are both atheistic. Where does this pessimistic interpretative scheme come from? The evidence suggests that it comes from French right-wing intellectuals, and more specifically from Jacques Maritain out of Charles Maurras. Maurras, an atheist and founder of the monarchist *Action Française* movement, declared in the early years of the century that French (and by extension, European) culture was corrupted by three factors that could conveniently be labelled the three R's: the Reformation – individualism in religion; Rationalism – private judgement now extended into the sphere of philosophy; and Romanticism – the overweening self-assertion of the ego. The remedy was to be a return to classical (i.e. Roman) discipline and sobriety.

Like almost everyone else, Maritain quarrelled with Maurras. Indeed, his title and slogan, *The Primacy of the Spiritual*, was specifically directed against Maurras who believed in '*La politique d'abord*' ('Politics is in command'). Yet in Maritain's book, *The Three Reformers* (first published in French by Spes in 1925), Maurras's account of European history is almost slavishly followed, except that Maritain names the enemy. His three 'reformers' turn out to be, not surprisingly, pseudo-reformers, in fact heretics. His book is devoted to Martin Luther, who expressed the anarchic individualism of the Reformation; René Descartes, who, good Catholic though he was, prefigures the rationalism of the 'so-called Enlightenment'; and Jean-Jacques Rousseau, whose misty *rêveries* and subjectivism anticipate the whole Romantic movement. Maritain is simply Maurras with the evidence provided. The conclusion of both is that there is nothing very much worth *praising* in Europe's last four hundred years. John Paul agrees with this conclusion – with a nuance that will be mentioned later.

What does it matter, it might be asked, what various Frenchmen, largely unknown outside specialist circles, thought on probably unanswerable questions about the course of European intellectual history? It matters because, if adopted by a reigning pope, who then sets these ideas in the wider context of his own apocalyptic sense that the world is a battlefield between Good and Evil, some very practical consequences will follow. Here is John Paul, tilting against Karl Rahner's theory of 'anonymous Christians':

> Atheism advocates the disappearance of all religion, but it is itself a religious phenomenon. But let us not, on that account, turn the atheist into a believer who is unaware of the fact [*un croyant qui s'ignore*]. And let us not turn a *profound drama* into a *superficial misunderstanding*. (10 October 1980)

This is one of the most revealing phrases uttered by John Paul. We can ignore the fact (while regarding it as unfortunate) that he completely caricatures the position of Rahner and other theologians who have written about 'anonymous Christians', and who certainly do not regard atheism as 'a superficial misunderstanding'. John Paul does not want to be deprived of his 'profound drama'. He wants his atheist to be a Prometheus-like figure, defying the gods to do their worst. He is not interested in a logical positivist atheist who is more likely to be pushing his bicycle up a hill than stealing fire from the gods. That there was a Promethean element in nineteenth-century atheism is beyond doubt. Marx said that 'Man is the supreme being for man' and Nietzsche's *Ecce Homo* can supply as much bombastic blasphemy as anyone requires.

John Paul's sense of the *dramatic* nature of the conflict between the atheist and the believer owes something to a book first published in 1944, Henri de Lubac's *Le Drame de l'Humanisme Athée* (Spes, Paris, 1944. Eng. tr. *The Drama of Atheistic Humanism*, Sheed and Ward, London, 1949). De Lubac was quoted in the address to the 'Atheism and Evangelization' conference:

'True, man can organize the world apart from God, but
without God man can organize it in the end only to man's
detriment. An isolated humanism is an inhuman humanism.' Four decades later, each of us can fill out these
prophetic words of Fr de Lubac with all the tragic burden
of our age. (10 October 1980. Paul VI had already used
this de Lubac quotation in his encyclical *Populorum
Progressio*, No. 42)

The comment implies that the drama has, if anything,
intensified since 1944. But if the typical atheist is a
Nietzschian Marxist of pronounced Promethean tendencies,
clearly there is nothing to be learned from him, and the
atheist becomes what he once reassuringly was: an enemy to
be combated and overcome.

Moreover, an added dimension of drama is injected when
one adds that in this battle between Good and Evil, the Devil
has a part to play. In the 'Atheism and Evangelization'
address John Paul speaks of modern man as 'enclosed within
himself and oscillating between Luciferian pride and
disillusioning despair'. In the retreat which he gave to the
Roman Curia in 1976, Cardinal Wojtyla dwelt at length on
the temptation of the serpent in the Book of Genesis, and
concluded from its third chapter ('You shall be as gods'):

It becomes clear that the whole history of mankind, and
with it the history of the world with which man is united
through the work of divine creation, will be subject both to
rule by the Word and the anti-Word, the Gospel and the
anti-Gospel. (*Sign of Contradiction,* St Paul Publications,
Slough, 1979, p. 29)

It is this on-going, perpetual and dramatic conflict that John
Paul detects behind the shimmering skein of contemporary
philosophical activity, through what he calls 'the crossfire of
pragmatist, neo-positivist, existentialist, marxist, structural-
ist, nietzschian atheism' (10 October 1980).

It would be otiose to spell out in detail what John Paul means by these six adjectives. They are not used with any great precision. They are not descriptive of what actually goes on where philosophical activity occurs. John Paul uses broad brush strokes which gloss over the details; but quite clearly they amount to disapproval of most of what happens in the name of philosophy. This poses a problem for some of the intellectuals whom John Paul wishes to woo. They are accustomed to a rational approach to philosophical problems, to stating a case, defining alternative positions, producing evidence, giving examples of the implications – all according to the excellent (though largely unacknowledged) principles of St Thomas Aquinas. John Paul disconcerts them by substituting for a rational approach an oracular argument from authority. But an argument from authority, however eminent the authority, does not count in philosophy.

It appears, however, to count in some Roman universities and in the Secretariat for Non-believers. The latter body was set up by Paul VI to engage in dialogue with unbelievers. It has now become in effect the secretariat for apologetics. It recently devoted an entire number of its bulletin to Galileo, who was certainly no unbeliever. The Urbanian University in Rome has also caught the new mood. It organized the conference already mentioned (Atheism and Evangelization), gathered a thousand participants, and said that its aim was 'to challenge atheism which today must be considered the number one problem for Christians whether in East or West . . . Atheism is today what paganism was for the early Church.' Fr Battista Mondin, director of the project, said quite explicitly that the time had come to 'move over to the offensive' and to cast aside all inferiority complexes because – this refrain is now becoming familiar – 'We are entering a period when other cultural forces are revealing their limitations, and there is strong evidence of a religious revival.'

However, not all intellectuals have so enthusiastically

joined in the new crusade. They might wish to make the following observations. Granted that John Paul has vividly described one particular type of atheist, are there not other atheists who are not necessarily anti-theist? Is not the commonest phenomenon, at least in the West, not so much aggressive atheism but an agnosticism, sometimes a 'reverent agnosticism', which is unable to conclude whether the chessboard is black or white? And does not the harsh alternative proposed by John Paul represent a rejection of the pontificates of John XXIII and Paul VI as well as of the Council itself?

In *Pacem in Terris* John XXIII made a distinction between 'the one who errs' and his 'error'. The person always retains his human dignity, and must be treated accordingly, even though his error is to be reproved (No. 158). Picking up this hint, the Council went further and recognized that 'the Church has greatly profited by the history and development of humanity' (*Gaudium et Spes*, No. 44). But if the world has gone astray since the Renaissance, it is difficult to see in what way the Church has 'profited' from what was going on. It is even more difficult to comprehend how the Church 'has greatly profited and still greatly profits from the antagonism of those who oppose or persecute her' (ibid.). No doubt this now proscribed tradition will go underground. Meanwhile enough conformist intellectuals – Italians or members of Opus Dei – can be wheeled out for international congresses where they will put their hands on their hearts and declare that the pontiff is not only right, but is also supremely wise, perceptive, far-sighted, and so on.

That is no caricature. Professor Augusto del Noce, of the University of Rome, will have to stand as a representative of the class. He gave the inaugural lecture at the UCIP (*Union Catholique Internationale de la Presse*) Congress held in Rome, 23–26 September 1980. He was barely intelligible, but in so far as he was he seemed to be echoing the analysis of European history offered by John Paul. In his own inimitable words:

We must think of the two faces of the Enlightenment: the Promethean and the Orphic. The Promethean is well-known: it has its symbol in the Baconian subservience of knowledge to power . . . Especially in recent years, that particular, romanticist reaction has gained ground which revives the old myth of primeval paradise whence man supposedly detached himself because of the erroneous path he has been following starting at least with Plato . . . It is not my intention at this point to dwell on this position, however I seem to see in it the shambles of classical German philosophy, from Hölderlin on. (mss. p. 3)

I apologize for wasting space with this farrago. It is merely the prelude to a vituperative attack on the 'Catholic press' which has stupidly bought the myth of progress. Moreover, in his final section, headed 'The Teachings of Pope Wojtyla', he actually says that 'the decisive turning point at which we stand is not between politico-social revolution and fascism, but a fight for God or against God which is clearly at the same time a fight for man or against him'. We are back to Italy 1937, and the so-called theological justification for fascism. With friends like del Noce, John Paul doesn't need enemies.

The reader may have the impression that intellectuals spend all their time at conferences discussing the 'crisis of civilization'. They do. No better definition could be found than that they are people with the time and inclination to discuss such weighty themes.

Just one more conference and we can move on. Addressing the conference on 'The Christian Roots of the European Nations', which he had prompted, he showed himself to be moderately optimistic or, at least, not quite so pessimistic. He claimed that there was an *alternative tradition* to the anti-God mainstream tradition. He talked about 'those great souls' (or 'great spirits') who alone are capable of saving Europe from catastrophe. Who are they? The whole remarkable paragraph must be given:

Europe needs Christ! It is necessary to enter into contact with him, lay hold of his message, his love, his eternal and exalting certainties! We have to understand that the Church willed and founded by him has as its only purpose to transmit and guarantee the truth revealed by him, and keep alive and relevant today the means of salvation he instituted, that is, the sacraments and prayer. This was grasped by chosen and thoughtful spirits such as Pascal, Newman, Rosmini, Soloviev and Norwid. (6 November 1981)

It was rather like a quiz question: what have these great spirits in common? Closer inspection proves rather discouraging. The extent of Blaise Pascal's 'Jansenism' is still being debated by scholars. Antonio Rosmini's book *The Five Wounds of the Church* was put on the *Index of Forbidden Books*. John Henry Newman was under a cloud during the pontificate of Pius IX because he thought that the definition of papal infallibility was inopportune and would have harmful results. The two Slavs escaped censure. Vladimir Soloviev was an Orthodox lay theologian who became a Roman Catholic. Cyprian Norwid is a nineteenth-century Polish poet who is said to have influenced Wojtyla's own youthful poetry. The quintet do not have the solidity one has the right to expect from 'chosen and thoughtful spirits'. They seem to be used rather like counters in an intellectual game.

Everything John Paul says to and about intellectuals presupposes the vanished world of the 1930s and 1940s. The atmosphere is that of Kraków revisited. It was a time when Catholics dreamed of a 'second renaissance' which, unlike the first, would realize a harmonious fusion of reason and faith, of art and faith. *'Refaire la renaissance'* was the motto of Emmanuel Mounier and his friends when they founded the review, *Esprit*, in 1932. It had considerable influence in Poland. Indeed, Renaissance (*Odrodzenie*) was the name of a pre-war Catholic movement in Poland and many of

Wojtyla's friends belonged to it. But in order to have a renaissance, you need renaissance men and women, that is all-rounders who can turn their hand to anything, from a sonnet to a sonata, from a philosophical essay to a dramatic dialogue. So Karol Wojtyla, the would-be actor now turned priest, continued to write poetry under the pseudonym of Andrzej Jawień, composed his play *Before the Jeweller's Shop*, and burned the midnight oil to complete his major philosophical work, *The Acting Person*.

Elsewhere in Europe, the 'Catholic Renaissance', as an ideal and a dream, faded and vanished from view: Catholics became more concerned with 'reforming the Church'. But in Poland the Catholic Renaissance ideal was kept alive, put on ice, as it were, in the communist refrigerator, so much so that when Karol Wojtyla became Pope in October 1978, what he had to say stirred nostalgic thoughts among the intellectuals who remembered their lost youth. They had been provided with a pessimistic view of European history, and their sense that atheism was on the advance was now confirmed by the highest authority in the Church. 'Atheism,' the Pope had said, 'has invaded the world of culture and the world of work' (10 October 1980). We have seen 'the world of culture'. Now we must turn to 'the world of work', with apologies to all those women who are either intellectuals or workers or both.

9

Solidarity with the Workers

John Paul II has the unique distinction of being the first pope who has had some experience of industrial work. From September 1940 to August 1944 he worked in the stone quarry attached to the Solvay chemical works in Kraków. One of his tasks was to carry buckets of lime on a yoke placed across his shoulders. The work was physically exhausting, and made doubly so by the inadequate diet of wartime Poland. No one could call these ordinary working conditions.

Fr Wojtyla set down some of his memories of working life in one of his finest poems, *The Quarry*, written in 1956, the year of the 'Polish spring'. Its final section is dedicated to a fellow worker who had been crushed to death. It is far from being a complacently clerical or facile poem. It blazes with anger at the apparent futility of his death. It ends:

> The stones on the move again: a wagon bruising
> the flowers.
> Again the electric current cuts deep into the walls.
> But the man has taken with him the world's inner
> structure,
> Where the greater the anger, the greater the
> explosion of love.
> (*Easter Vigil and Other Poems*, translated by
> Jerzy Peterkiewicz, Hutchinson, 1979, p. 33)

In 1956 Stanislaw Gomulka, after a spell in Stalin's prisons, became First Secretary of the Polish Communist Party. There was much talk of 'the Polish road to socialism' which was an assertion of relative autonomy but within the tight framework provided by the Soviet Union.

In 1957 Wojtyla published two more 'industrial' poems. The first, *The Car Factory Worker*, expresses a mood of deep 'alienation'. The worker cannot 'put himself into his work' which is taken over and exploited by someone else. This is usually a Marxist complaint about capitalist industries. But for Wojtyla, the fact of changing the owners and substituting state capitalism for private capitalism did nothing to improve the situation. So the worker complains:

> I am not with them at the controls
> on sleek motorways; the policeman's in charge.
> They stole my voice; it's the cars that speak.
>
> (ibid., p. 40)

The second 'industrial' poem of 1957 is about an armaments factory worker who suffers from an inability to see where his work is leading. This is another form of 'alienation' – but ironical this time, because of what he is making:

> I only turn screws, weld together
> parts of destruction,
> never grasping the whole,
> or the human lot.
>
> (ibid., p. 41)

These themes – love overcoming anger, and alienation – will later reappear in developed form in the encyclicals *Redemptor Hominis* and *Laborem exercens*. They are more vivid in their original source.

Nor can it plausibly be argued that young Fr Wojtyla was patronizing the workers or romanticizing his experience of work. He knew what he was talking about, even though, as time went on, the impact of his experience in the quarry faded and became, in Newman's phrase, 'the memory of a memory'. But even as Archbishop of Kraków, he was not isolated from working-class life. In much of 'continental' Europe the Church was alleged to have 'lost the workers' and forgotten how to talk to 'urban man'; and guilt feelings accompanied this failure. But this never happened in Poland. In the nineteenth century, when the country was carved up between its three powerful neighbours, Prussia, Russia and Austria-Hungary, the Church kept alive the aspirations of the Polish people. In Lodz, then a textiles city, there were stirrings of a Catholic 'social movement'. At the great Marian shrines it was said: 'Here, Our Lady speaks Polish.' So no wedge could be driven between workers and clergy. The solidarity of the clergy with the people was reinforced in the Second World War when over 2000 priests were executed or perished in concentration camps. This was one of the reasons why the Communist Party found it difficult to prise apart the people and the Church. In Hungary, where the Church had been a great landowner, the task was relatively easy, given patience and cunning. In Poland it failed.

As Pope, John Paul tends to assume that what was true in Poland will be verified elsewhere, and that it is possible to talk of 'work' and the 'workers' in general. Of course he admits that some distinctions have to be made. Alongside the heavy industries that characterized the 'first' industrial revolution – engineering, shipbuilding, mining – are the 'service' industries and the cleaner, computer-based activities which depend on the micro-chip. This is recognized in *Laborem exercens*. But there is another form of work, more ancient and fundamental, which John Paul values greatly and puts in a category apart: agriculture.

On all his international journeys John Paul has addressed 'peasants' or their equivalents: at Des Moines in the United States they turned out to be farming millionaires with original Picassos on the walls of their split-level houses. But they all receive the same message. Agriculture is privileged because it fulfils, in a direct way, the command of Genesis to 'subdue the earth':

Man subdues the earth much more when he begins to cultivate it and then transform its products, adapting them to his own use. Thus agriculture constitutes through human work a *primary field* of economic activity and an indispensable factor of production. (*Laborem exercens*, No. 5)

In the beginning was the man with a hoe, the man with a spade, nowadays the man with a combine harvester. And whatever the complexities of modern civilization, agriculture retains its fundamental place. For unless we can feed ourselves on spaceship earth, we have no future at all. This is a theme that John Paul has stressed in his messages to FAO (the United Nations Food and Agriculture Organization) which is the 'other' international body to have its headquarters in Rome.

The emphasis on the role of the 'peasant' also makes an anti-Marxist point. For Marx the 'typical' worker, the one whose 'consciousness' could be raised, was the industrial worker. Marx was not much interested in the farm labourer. And in practice communism has been singularly unsuccessful in its dealings with peasants – either murdering them off through forced collectivization (Stalin and the *kulaks*) or leaving them to their own devices as in Poland where 80 per cent of the land remains in the hands of small-holders. No more will be said about peasants here, except that John Paul exhorts them to hold fast to traditional ways and that he thinks, in the manner of Georges Sand, that they are somehow 'closer to nature'. In Kisangani (formerly Stanleyville), Zaire, he presented a portrait of Jesus as a countryman:

He carefully observed nature and loved it deeply, the flowers and the trees, the seasons, work in the fields, the work of the ploughman, the reaper, the shepherd, the vine-grower, the woman who goes to the well for water, who prepares the bread and the meals. He knew the

local customs which mark out the rhythms of local life.
(6 May 1980)

Kisangani, on the River Zaire, is surrounded by fairly
impenetrable jungle, and in that setting this idyllic picture of
life down on the farm seemed very Europe-centred. But there
were some very biblical-looking fishermen on the river.

It is the industrial worker who has, as they say, the muscle.
John Paul has devoted much time to industrial workers. He
has gradually improved his technique in dealing with them.
To illustrate this I shall consider three meetings with
workers: Pomezia, Italy (13 September 1979); Paris (31 May
1980); and Terni, Italy (19 March 1981). By the time of this
last meeting, all the elements of *Laborem exercens*, the
encyclical on work, had already been tried out.

The Pomezia meeting was, to be frank, a near-disaster. It
is a new town between Castelgandolfo and the sea. It has
expanded rapidly – from a village of 1500 in 1939 to its
present 30,000. Unemployment is high. Many of its 256
factories have locked their gates; some are occupied by the
workers. Only about 8000 people turned up for the Pope's
visit – Vatican sources had predicted 50,000. The local
Bishop censored the speech of welcome by a local trades
union leader, Eurosia Zagaria. She was not allowed to
mention the strikes and the sit-ins. John Paul ploughed
dutifully through his prepared speech. The first mild
applause came when he said that 'work is made for man, not
man for work'. *Unità*, the communist daily, liked John
Paul's anti-capitalist remarks: 'We are well beyond the first
and primitive stage of the industrial revolution, when people
believed that social harmony would result from the mere
interplay of market forces.' John Paul concluded his speech
with a novel ending: 'In the name of the Lord I bless you all
and shake your hand fraternally.' It was so cold and formal,
rather like the visit of minor royalty.

In the end, John Paul saved the day by his subsequent
impromptu remarks. He talked of his own time in the Solvay

chemical works in Kraków. He said the years spent as a worker were of greater value to him than two university doctorates. He apologized for the vagueness of his prepared speech, attributing it to ignorance of local conditions. He promised to come again. On receiving the gift of a silver salver from the employers' association, he joked: 'How can there be social justice if you insist on making the Pope so rich?' So John Paul won over the crowd gradually. But the lessons of Pomezia were mostly negative. A future meeting with the workers would need better preparation on the local level and some direct involvement of the Pope with the workers themselves.

If Pomezia was a sighting-shot, it was expected that the homily at the basilica of Saint Denis in Paris would be a major statement on the world of work. Once the burial place of French kings, Saint Denis is now a working-class suburb with a high proportion of immigrants. Many of them were waiting outside in the square, along with the communist mayor of Saint Denis. They saw a large banner proclaiming the slogan of Cardinal Joseph Cardijn, founder of the Young Christian Workers: 'A young worker is worth all the gold in the world.' Rather curiously, the liturgy took place inside the basilica, but the homily was outside on the square. It soon became apparent that homily and liturgy were not moving in the same direction.

The specially prepared liturgy reflected the leftward move of the French Church in the last decade. It breathed fire and defiance against capitalism. The opening penitential rite included the following tough-minded observation:

> In our region jobs are suppressed, immigrants are expelled, rights are threatened, and our children are denied a future – all for profit. We have not banded together to demand justice. Jesus Christ, forgive our lack of unity, forgive our lack of courage.

That did not sound very repentant. The intercessions evoked

the plight of the Métro cleaners who had been on strike for twenty-one days. The first words assigned to the Pope to read were: 'You are a people who struggles for a better future, a people who suffers and hopes.'

How would John Paul respond to this left-wing rhetoric? He began by denouncing abortion: this was the Feast of the Annunciation and the text about Elisabeth's child leaping in the womb proved irresistible. The communist mayor cheered up a little when John Paul moved on to the dignity of work. But his next move was disconcerting. John Paul looked at work in terms of the family and said:

> When a man works to ensure the subsistence of his family, then he puts into his work all the daily fatigue of his love . . . It is true that he can also love work for its own sake, because it allows him to share in the task of subduing the earth, willed by the Creator. But the love that a man puts into his work is only really complete if he is bound and united with others, and above all with those who are his own flesh. (31 May 1980)

That is not what is usually meant by 'working-class solidarity' (and not what *Solidarnosc* meant either). The passage also seems to imply that although work can be loved for its own sake, this will be a rare event: alienation is the ordinary state, and so work has to find its justification outside itself. It is good if it is *for* others. Teilhard de Chardin persuaded a whole generation (and the Council too) that work has an *intrinsic* value; at Saint Denis John Paul declared that it had (only?) an extrinsic value.

This is why he yokes together family and work:

> The rights of the family should be written into the very foundation of the work code, which should be concerned with man, and not just with production or profit. How, for example, can we find a satisfactory solution to the problem of women working in factories, often at an

107

exhausting pace, who feel they should be at home with their husband and children?

But the main social problem in Saint Denis is not so much working wives: it concerns rather those immigrant workers who are allowed to come in to do the menial jobs the French will not do, but who are not allowed to bring in their wives. (I will return to the subject of working wives in the next chapter.) Perhaps it was inadequate briefing: but there was a distinct feeling of minds not meeting.

Misunderstanding continued when John Paul proceeded to 'spiritualize' the concept of 'struggle'. The term is much more used in the Latin languages, sounds much tougher (*lutte*, *lucha*, *lotta*, etc.), and is usually accompanied by an upraised, clenched fist. It refers to the class struggle. At Saint Denis John Paul took over this language and said that workers today 'should be capable of struggling nobly for every kind of justice, for the true good of man, for all the rights of the human person, the family, the nation and humanity'. That sounded like a firm commitment to the struggle, all the more when he quoted the Magnificat's vehement denunciation of the rich. But then came the qualification:

> Yet this thirst for justice, this eagerness to struggle for the truth and the moral order of the world, is not and cannot be founded on hatred, nor should it be a source of hatred in the world. (ibid.)

This was a very clear rejection of the class war on the very sensible grounds that while you can build constructively on love, hatred and the labelling of others ('capitalist', 'enemy of the working-class', etc.) lead to intolerance, tyranny and injustice. At the same time one has to ask whether the attempt to steal the Marxist clothes and make struggle mean 'the struggle for justice' can really succeed.

The visit to the massive steel works at Terni, north of Rome, on the Feast of St Joseph, 19 March 1981, raised the

same question. But this time there was a real attempt
genuinely to 'meet the workers'. John Paul was shown round
the plant wearing a steel helmet inscribed Giovanni Paulo II.
Inevitably it reminded him of the Lenin Steel Works at
Nowa Huta. Two local factors helped to make the day a
success. First, the Bishop of Terni, Santo Quadri, has long
been interested in social problems and had devoted his
pastoral letter the previous Christmas to the local industrial
crisis. Secondly, relations between Christians and communists have been good in Terni, and the mayor who
welcomed John Paul is a communist.

Whatever the reason, John Paul's speech at the factory
gate was better received than any of his previous attempts to
address the workers:

> I agree with you about the sad fact of unemployment,
> about the tedium of factory work, and the importance of
> stressing that when work alienates man and stunts his
> growth, then it is anti-human work and the worker
> remains a slave.
>
> I agree also that it is intolerable that military arsenals
> should be filled with frightening nuclear weapons, bearers
> of death and destruction, while millions of human
> creatures die of hunger . . . Be assured that the Pope is with
> you, that the Pope is on your side, whenever justice has
> been violated, peace is threatened or the due rights of
> every one and the common good need to be encouraged.
> (19 March 1981)

It might be thought that this is all rather vague, that it
communicates attitudes rather than ideas, and that it did
not commit John Paul to anything in particular. His next
remarks were an attempt to answer that objection:

> I know concretely the difficulties that characterize
> working conditions in the dioceses of Terni, Narni and
> Amélia. The sackings, social security problems, the down-

turn in profitability are all facts which, although not the result of ill-will, nevertheless represent objectively a threat for many families and require an attentive and close examination of their true causes and possible solutions.

However, it was not the function of the Church to undertake this detailed study or to propose solutions. It functions on a different level. It asks fundamental questions. It offers criteria for judgement.

But the most important event at Terni was still to come. John Paul had a question-and-answer session with the works council, and later sat down to lunch in the works canteen. Toasts were drunk in red wine. The informal session began nervously enough, with no one wishing to be the first to speak. John Paul helped them out: 'This reminds me of the place where I used to work during the war. The atmosphere and the work were very different, but the human climate was very similar. I think I have grasped that your greatest worry, these days, is about job security. Am I right about this?' It was simple. It was effective. The exchanges began to come thick and fast. Here are three of them.

'You said that we are the bosses in the factory [*i padroni della fabrica*]. But the truth is that we cannot decide anything. You have come to us today. But tomorrow we are going to Rome for a demo. It's not against you, we're glad you've come. It's against the government that completely ignores our feelings.'

'This talk of love and solidarity is all very well, but we know perfectly well that our problems can only be solved through struggle, through, in fact, the class struggle.'

'When you worked in the factory, did you ever feel a vocation to become a trades union leader?'

For the first time in his pontificate, John Paul had to listen before speaking. And for the first time he was without a prepared script, in a language that is not his own. These impromptu replies reveal far more of the man than elaborate philosophical ideas developed in *Laborem exercens*.

Moving to the green baize table, he explained what he had meant by saying that 'the workers are the bosses':

> This is a principle of social ethics that the Church has always held. It is the workers who are the principal cause of production, and, because they are human persons, they are not an instrument to be used by others. Other things are instruments, but they are not, for they are men, and they are the primary and substantial cause of what they produce. And so they have the right to the fruits of their labour. That means not only a fair wage, but a certain sharing in the management of the firm, and a share in the profitables. Have I got the right Italian word?

He had not. But no one minded. 'Keep right on,' they shouted.

His treatment of the question about the 'class war' echoed what he had said in Paris. First he declared himself delighted that the word 'struggle' had been mentioned, because one has to struggle for justice. But care must be taken that this 'struggle' should not become a struggle *against* individuals or groups. Positively, the struggle for justice means

> a greater sensitivity to what is justice for the working-class, which is linked, in my view, with justice according to the Gospel. The Church seeks a more just world, an ever more just world, and all those who share in this struggle walk the way of the Gospel, walk the way of Christian doctrine.

But that is precisely what the theory of 'anonymous Christians', so rudely dismissed in the last chapter, was trying to say. Coherence is not the strong suit of this pontificate. Happily.

Finally John Paul confessed that the thought of becoming a trades union leader had never crossed his mind. His vocation had been a different one from the outset. But, he added, 'I think the vocation of defending one's fellow workers is wonderful. In essence it is a Christian vocation. Anyway, some of my compatriots have discovered a vocation to be trades unionists, notably Lech Walesa.' This brought thunderous applause because Walesa's first journey outside Poland had been to Italy in the previous January. Though invited and funded by the Italian unions, Walesa did not disguise the fact that he had gone to Italy chiefly to meet and thank the Pope.

So the visit to the Terni steel works came to an end. As he left, John Paul overheard a television reporter saying to camera: 'This is the first time a pope has eaten with the workers.' John Paul paused a moment and said privately: 'And that's not the only novelty of this pontificate.'

This was on 19 March 1981. But for the shooting, *Laborem exercens* would have appeared on 15 May, two months later, ninetieth anniversary to the day of *Rerum Novarum*, the first ever 'social' encyclical. Evidently John Paul was working on it at the time he went to Terni. In the end it appeared on 15 September. It contains all the themes we have already seen in this chapter: the primacy of the person over things; a reluctance to endorse either capitalism or communism; the futility of the class war; the need to build a civilization on love; a determined search for a 'third way' that would be neither capitalism nor communism. There is no further need for summary here. But two comments are called for.

First, *Laborem exercens* is a deliberate attempt to revivify 'Catholic Social Doctrine'. His predecessor, Paul VI, had abandoned the idea as too grandiose. In *Octogesima Adveniens*, which commemorated the eightieth anniversary of *Rerum Novarum*, Paul VI had written:

In view of the varied situations in the world, it is difficult to give one teaching to cover them all or to offer a solution which has universal value. This is not our intention or even our mission. (*Octogesima Adveniens*, 14 May 1971, No. 4)

Ten years later John Paul II reveals no such inhibitions. The task that Paul VI felt unable and incompetent to fulfil he embarks upon with his customary *brio*.

But then he encounters along his path the difficulties which 'social doctrine' has always found. Either it confines itself to general principles, and then it remains in the stratosphere of platitudes: or else it is precise, and then it does not apply in every case. So, for example, John Paul is obviously right to say that the permanent and systematic opposition of capital and labour has the most damaging consequences. But how is this to be overcome? John Paul suggests that the way forward consists in 'proposals for the joint ownership of the means of work, sharing by the workers in the management and/or profit of businesses, so-called share-holding by labour, etc.' (No. 14). Again, these are perfectly sensible suggestions, but they suffer from the drawback that they have hardly ever been realized except, and then briefly, in Yugoslavia. So while one can present them as a good idea to be entertained, they can hardly be considered a major tenet of Catholic social doctrine. But the moment one says that, they can be ignored by all those who wish to ignore them. So the Pope's words are deprived of their cutting edge.

A similar problem arises when John Paul discusses what unions are for. He says that their main task 'is to defend the existential interests of workers in all sectors in which their rights are concerned' (No. 20). They have a social or welfare function. They should not 'play politics'. He explains:

> Unions do not have the character of political parties struggling for power; they should not be subjected to the decisions of political parties or have too close links with them. (No. 20)

This can be considered sound pragmatic advice for Solidarity in Poland: it was because some of its members forgot the first principle and overreached themselves that General Jaruzelski was given a pretext for moving so crushingly against Solidarity. Perhaps Solidarity should have heeded the Pope. But, on the other hand, the same principles applied strictly in Britain would mean the end of the political levy, no more sponsorship of Labour MPs by trades unions, and a refusal of TUC members to take part in the National Executive Committee meetings of the Labour Party and the annual Party Conference. Of course one is free to say that these do not constitute the 'too close links' with a political party of which the Pope speaks. But then his statement begins to 'die the death of a thousand qualifications'. It seems highly improbable that Pope John Paul will come to Britain and say to trades unionists: 'What have you done to implement *Laborem exercens*?' That illustrates the difficulty of Catholic 'social doctrine'.

10

The Other Half of Humanity

Pope John Paul II has been dogged by women. Some have pulled buttons off his white soutane or planted lipsticked kisses on his sleeve. Others have exercised the function of 'fraternal criticism' discussed in Chapter 1. There were three notable instances of women who followed the example of St Catherine of Siena, a fourteenth-century mystic who did not hesitate to give popes advice.

In Washington on 7 September 1979, Sr Teresa Kane, in her address of welcome to John Paul, diffidently drew attention to 'the intense suffering and pain that is part of the life of many women in the US Church'. She had heard what John Paul had to say about human rights, and she thought that this powerful message should have an impact within the Church itself. She was wearing a brown two-piece suit with a large lapel cross identifying her as a religious. She went on, gradually overcoming her evident nervousness:

> The Church in its struggle to be faithful to its call for reverence and dignity for all persons must respond by providing the possibility of women as persons being included in all the ministries of the Church.

The key word was *all*. That means 'including the priestly ministry'. Although Sr Teresa was later denounced as 'a publicity-seeking nun', her motives were sincere enough. She does not wish to be ordained herself. Later that afternoon she told me: 'I didn't mean to be dramatic, and I had prayed a great deal about this. I said what I had to say respectfully. I believe that dialogue is the best approach.'

In Philadelphia, a few days before, John Paul had said that 'the Church's traditional decision to call men to the priesthood, and not women, is not a statement about human rights, nor an exclusion of women from the holiness and mission of the Church' (4 October 1979). But it is an exclusion from ministry. Sr Teresa had brought up again a matter that had been resolved. John Paul must have had advance warning of what she was going to say. The proof is that he replied to her instantly in a passage that was manifestly added to his prepared address at the last moment.

John Paul presented Mary, the Mother of God, as '*the* woman of history and destiny'. But even Mary had her limitations, he explained, for she is 'the woman who is honoured as the Queen of the Apostles without herself being incorporated into the hierarchical constitution of the Church – yet she makes all hierarchy possible'. To make it quite clear that he was speaking of ordination, or rather of non-ordination, John Paul pointed out that Mary was not present at the Last Supper, though she was there at the foot of the cross. In other words the woman may suffer, but not minister. Her chains may be of gold, but they are none the less chains. It was eloquent enough, an appeal to piety against human rights, but it was not very convincing and was a good instance of that 'ideological manipulation' of theological concepts of which Christian feminists complain. A cartoon in *The National Catholic Reporter* summed it up with the caption: 'The Pope got it all wrong – he kissed the ground and trampled on the women' (19 October 1979).

Another encounter, much less publicized, with an outspoken nun took place in Paris on 3 June 1980, when John Paul met over 5000 French sisters in the garden of the rue du Bac 140, mother house of the Sisters of Charity and home of the 'miraculous medal'. (In 1830 Catherine Labouré, a novice from Burgundy, had a vision in which Our Lady directed her to have a medal struck which would have miraculous properties: and so it came to pass. Pius XII canonized her in 1947.) The address of welcome was given by Sr Danièle Souillard, a Handmaid of the Sacred Heart from Versailles. She too was in civilian dress, and she tried to explain why: 'For the sake of the Gospel our sisters are committed to justice and live among the least favoured. That is why our life-style has changed, and why we have changed our professional work and our dress' (*Le Monde*, 3 June 1980). John Paul pointedly ignored Sr Danièle's remarks and urged the sisters 'never to be ashamed to recognize clearly your identity as women consecrated to the Lord'. Some of them found this rather question-begging and insulting, as though they had given up the habit in order to get up to no good.

The third woman to rise up was not a religious. Barbara Engl is President of the Munich association of Catholic youth. On 20 November 1980, after a Mass in the bitterly cold Theresienwiese in Munich, she was due to say farewell to the Pope. After listening to his homily on Satan in our midst, she threw away her manuscript and spoke rapidly from a few hastily jotted down notes. 'Young people have the feeling,' she said, 'that the Church is more interested in perpetuating divisions with the Evangelical Church than in what brings us all together. They find that their concern for friendship, sexuality and partnership meets with only negative answers.' Ms Engl continued to pour out her heart as John Paul hid his head in his hands:

Many young people cannot understand why the Church should insist so strongly on celibacy for its priests, when there is an evident lack of priests and especially of young chaplains in high schools and universities. Nor can young people understand why a greater sharing of women in the ministry should be ruled out. We know perfectly well that the Gospel challenges us, but we do not feel oppressed by neurosis or a lack of courage because we know that Christ has promised us the fullness of life. (*Süddeutsche Zeitung*, 20 November 1980)

It was the most trenchant and comprehensive critique to date. John Paul made no reply. He was late, and he was hustled away by Cardinal Joseph Ratzinger, Archbishop of Munich, who ought not to have let this happen.

After Germany precautions were taken to ensure that there were no more maverick women around to disturb the harmony of papal journeys. Women like Mrs Imelda Marcos, wife of the perpetual President of the Philippines, took over. Each time John Paul stepped out of the plane in his island-hopping journey round the archipelago, Imelda, the first lady, cool and beautiful, was there to greet him, dressed in a peach or pink robe, elegantly handling her multi-coloured parasol. She explained her ubiquity by saying that it was an old Filipino custom that the lady of the household should welcome illustrious guests. It also did no harm to her chances of succeeding her husband. That was in February 1981.

So there was a transition from woman as challenge to woman as the object of chivalry. John Paul was much happier with that. For chivalry was part of the culture of the late Austro-Hungarian Empire. No guest arrived without flowers for the lady of the household; and on arrival he bowed low and kissed her hand (unless he was a priest, in which case such behaviour would be scandalous). These customs have survived communism and economic privation. They may not survive martial law.

It should be added that in this tradition there is no prejudice against women being learned. John Paul would agree with St Thomas More about the importance of higher education for women. The co-founder of the University of Kraków in the fifteenth century, Queen Hedwiga, was considerably more cultivated then her rather rough-grained husband. Intellectual women have always had a place in modern Poland: Marie Curie is the most famous woman scientist of all time. And in the Catholic circles of Kraków, particularly in the *Znak* (Sign) movement, there have been and still are lay theologians of considerable distinction. It was a woman (admittedly in exile) who undertook the daunting task of editing the English version of John Paul's philosophical work, *The Acting Person*. Anna-Teresa Tymieniecka's contribution has been variously interpreted. The point is that the concept of chivalry does not imply any lack of intellectual equality or achievement. But it does imply a difference. What sort of difference? John Paul's answer is that there is a physical and biological difference which carries with it a psychological difference. For some this will be a truism; for others a shattering blow.

John Paul's thinking on these matters starts from the Book of Genesis: 'Male and female he created them' (Genesis 1:27b). The differences between men and women are not accidental or culturally conditioned. They are rather based on God's plan for mankind. They are *significant* differences. They are, as it were, built in. Several consequences follow from this starting point.

First it involves a rejection of the 'sociological' approach to the problem, which sets aside or underestimates biological and physical differences. The 'sociological' approach does not talk about the 'nature' of men and women, in which it does not believe, but rather about the social roles that either men or women can play. In simpler terms: either of them can do the shopping, the cooking, the cleaning, the washing up, the child care. None of these activities belongs more to women than to men. So the interchangeability of roles is proclaimed as the test of true equality and a mature relationship between the sexes. Thus it is argued that if maternity leave exists, then paternity leave ought also to exist. John Paul opposes this tendency because he believes that the differences between men and women reveal something about God's deeper intention for mankind.

John Paul appeals to Jung for evidence that male and female are not just chance categories or neutral facts that can be set aside as indifferent. They act as 'archetypes' or *Urbilder*, i.e. basic and synthetic perceptions or images out of which we build up our picture of the universe as a whole

(12 March 1980 with reference to *Eranos* 6, 1938, C. J. Jung, 'The Psychological Aspects of the Maternal Archetype'). They condition our way of grasping ourselves and the world. 'According to this view,' says John Paul, 'the mutual man-woman relationship is itself an archetype based on the awareness that humanity is twofold, male and female' (ibid.).

John Paul's description of femininity involves three interrelated elements: biology, maternity and mystery. All three come together in the following passage:

> The mystery of femininity is manifested and finally revealed in maternity, as our text says, 'She conceived and gave birth' [Genesis 4:1]. Woman appears before man as the mother, at the origin of a new human life which is conceived and developed in her and thus born into the world. This also unveils the mystery of masculinity in so far as he is the generator of new life.
>
> The theology of the body contained in the Book of Genesis is concisely and briefly expressed. Yet we find in it fundamental concepts that are in some sense primary and definitive. Everything is contained in the biblical term 'knowledge' ('The man *knew* his wife Eve, and she conceived', 4:1). The physical make-up of woman differs from that of the male; and today we know so much more about the bio-physiological aspects of this difference. This is externally manifested up to a point in the appearance and form of the body. Maternity reveals this constitution from within as a special capacity of the female organism which has the creative power to conceive and give birth to a human being, with the help of man. (12 March 1980)

Various conclusions flow from this kind of discourse. The first is that, as Freud observed, 'biology is destiny'. With this starting point one will want to maintain the specific differences between male and female and confirm them by insisting on distinct and separate roles. This is the fundamental ground for John Paul's opposition to the ordination of women. It is the reason why he is opposed to homosexual activity, male or female, which by definition blurs, confuses or destroys traditional sexual roles and cannot lead to paternity or maternity.

This approach also justifies talk about 'mystery' which is partly a cultural tradition and partly the sense, found in the Bible but still available today, of sheer wonder at the origin of life. The theme of 'the mystery of woman', Goethe's 'eternal feminine', common in the Romantic movement, was found in many Catholic writers such as Coventry Patmore, Charles Péguy and Paul Claudel. To allow symbolic meanings to play on the edge of consciousness seemed to them an antidote to cold rationalism. And the 'mystery' of womanhood culminates in Mary, the Mother of God, '*the* woman of history and destiny', the Second Eve.

If one is going to think about woman in this way, one will probably assign to her or impose on her a set of 'feminine characteristics', perhaps even a 'feminine nature'. One woman who has attracted John Paul's attention, though not for her 'fraternal correction' of his predecessors, is St Catherine of Siena. She died on 29 April 1380. Six hundred years later to the day John Paul preached a homily on her in which he said:

> Her feminine nature was richly endowed with fantasy, intuition, sensibility, an ability to get things done, a capacity to communicate with others, a readiness for self-giving and service. (29 April 1980)

That sounds like a compliment, but it also has the effect of keeping women in their subordinate place. The first three qualities mentioned are ambivalent: ah! the sweet dears, so imaginative, so sensitive, intuiting and twittering away, how we love 'em! The curious thing is that no one ever attempts to define the 'masculine nature' or even to address 'males' as a separate category.

121

Now the question arises: supposing we accept the obvious biological differences between men and women and agree that these archetypal differences carry an important symbolic potential for poets, lovers, mystical theologians and Jungian psychiatrists. What else follows? What practical consequences ensue? Does this in the end simply mean that women should be confined to the church, the kitchen and the children (as the expressive German phrase, *Kinder, Kirche, Küche,* puts it)?

This is not an easy question to answer, because every time John Paul speaks on this subject he carefully does not say that 'women should stay at home' but rather insists that women 'should not be *forced* to work outside the home' against their will. In this way he is seen to be fighting in a good cause. And since in Poland women have been forced to work without any change in the division of domestic tasks, most working women now do two jobs instead of one. John Paul springs chivalrously to their defence, not by saying that their husbands should share in domestic tasks and child care, but by saying that they should not be compelled to work outside the home at all. Two recent (1981) films by Polish women, J. Kamienska's *Working Women* and K. Kwinta's *The White Women,* are a searing indictment of the conditions of Dickensian squalor in which many Polish women have to work. In this context, to talk of going to work as a 'liberation' must seem merely a sinister joke. But in this matter the Polish experience is limited.

It seemed reasonable to expect that the 1980 Synod on the family would find time to discuss the place of women in society. In his final address to the Synod, John Paul replied to some of the points that had been made. He had one sentence on our question, which, for once, will be left in the ungainly gobbledygook of the official translation:

It is commendably asked that women should not be forced to engage in external work, proper to a certain role or, as they say, a profession, but rather that the family might be able to live rightly, that the mother might devote herself fully to the family. (25 October 1980)

John Paul here was not supposed to be presenting his own thoughts but summing up the advice given to him by the Synod. But this piece of advice chimed in so perfectly with his own known views that the suspicion grew that he was using the Synod as a sounding-board for his own ideas. By framing his statement in this way ('It is commendably asked'), however, John Paul appeared to be responding to some deep desire expressed by the Synod. Who, then, had said that working women neglect their families?

Research among the 162 speeches delivered at the Synod, and of the subsequent written submissions, revealed that 'the problem of women at work' was not a major concern. Not only that, but a large number of interventions emphasized that the time had come to take women seriously in the Church and in society. Archbishop Godefried Daneels, successor of Cardinal Léon-Joseph Suenens in Brussels-Malines, said that in the nineteenth century, the Church lost the workers because it neglected their rights: it was running a similar risk of losing women in the latter half of the twentieth century. Bishop Robert Lebel of Valleyfield, Canada, claimed that one of the Synod's achievements was that it had recognized that 'the feminist movement is a good thing and that it contains some Gospel values'. Bishop Lebel was faithfully reporting the Synod. Although this was not made public at the time, its final report contained the following comment:

By widespread tradition down to our day, woman's role was in the home, while man's was outside it. The movement for women's rights has shown us that the role of wife and mother is on an equal footing with public roles and certain professions. Besides, cultural and social evolution should cause these roles to influence each other . . . The Church can help today's society by examining

123

the value of housework and child-rearing, whether it is
done by husband or wife. (Proposition 16, in *The Tablet*,
31 January 1981, p. 118)

Nothing of this was reflected in John Paul's address at the
end of the Synod; nor is it reflected in *Familiaris Consortio*,
an apostolic exhortation which was his official and written
response to the Synod (15 December 1981).

There was, however, one speech at the Synod on which
John Paul could found his case against working wives. It
came from seventy-two-year-old Cardinal Egidio Vagnozzi,
formerly apostolic delegate in Washington and at the time of
his speech President of the Prefecture of Economic Affairs.
So he was a diplomat turned banker. He was to die the
following 26 December, St Stephen's Day. This was
therefore his swansong.

He began by saying that 'little or nothing has been said in
the Synod about married women who, with no real need,
work outside the home' (14 October 1980). This was an
interesting admission. It tells us that despite John Paul's
attempt to present his remarks as a *conclusion* of the Synod,
the topic was hardly discussed at all. Moreover it reveals a
very strange view of the world. Vagnozzi's concept of 'real
need' is very limited: if she doesn't need the money, she
should stay at home. It does not seem to have occurred to
him that the 'need' in question could be psychological, and
that the good of the family as a whole could depend upon the
mother having some interest or work outside the home. But
Cardinal Vagnozzi could only imagine two reasons why
women should work. Either they abandon home and family
'in order to increase unnecessarily the family income, seeking
only greater riches and comforts'; or they are driven to work
because of poverty or because, not having children, they look
for a job so as to have something to do with their time.
Vagnozzi's conclusion gives the game away completely: 'The
Synod must say something about this problem which
undermines family integrity and increases unemployment

among young and married men, thereby creating a serious social problem.' It was a perfect example of 'ideological' thinking. It purported to be making a theological statement when in fact it was defending the position of the male in our society. Vagnozzi's speech let the cat out of the bag.

Yet this speech was all John Paul had to rely on for his 'conclusion' to the Synod. Vagnozzi's speech was like a caricature of his own position. John Paul has returned to the topic of working women many times. In *Laborem exercens* he shows rather more subtlety than Vagnozzi – not a difficult feat. He writes:

> It will redound to the credit of society to make it possible for a mother – without inhibiting her freedom, without psychological or practical discrimination, and without penalizing her as compared with other women – to devote herself to taking care of her children and educating them in accordance with their needs, which vary with age. Having to abandon these tasks in order to take up paid work outside the home is wrong from the point of view of the good of the family when it contradicts or hinders these primary goals of the mission of a mother. (No. 19)

Through the cascade of qualifications, a number of points emerge. First, John Paul is not talking about women generally but about *mothers*. This is an important distinction: a woman does not have to be a wife and a mother, but once she is, one can concede that certain responsibilities follow. Next the admission that the needs of children vary with age permits another distinction. A better case can be made for a mother staying at home with toddlers than with teenagers (although she also needs respite from toddlers). The three 'without' clauses ('without inhibiting her freedom', etc.) are puzzling. They seem to be making a concession. The woman in the home would not be 'penalized' if, for example, there was some financial compensation for her not having a job outside. That could be done, to some extent, through family allowances or the 'family wage' which is mentioned in this same section.

John Paul defines 'the family wage' as 'a single salary given to the head of the family for his work, sufficient for the family, without the other spouse having to take up gainful employment outside' (No. 19). Quite clearly, from all we have seen, 'the head of the family' is the husband. In the ideal and socially just society envisaged by John Paul, the husband is the breadwinner and the mother the housewife. The roles are clear and traditional. No account is taken of Pope John XXIII's *Pacem in Terris* (1963), which speaks of 'the entry of women into public life' and 'women's growing sense of their dignity as human persons' as positive 'signs of the times'.

I have already hinted that the explanation of John Paul's attitudes is cultural rather than theological. But here the 'Polish factor' is relevant in a novel way. Jozefa Hennelowa in her portrait of Polish women (in *Nous Chrétiens de Pologne*, pp. 111–24) takes it for granted that they will be at work – and from six o'clock in the morning. So the Polish mother is *unable to perform the task the Pope wishes her to perform*. It is not that she does not want to do it: it is rather that she simply *cannot*. There are three ways of getting your children looked after: the state or factory nursery school; private foster mothers who are subject to no medical or other control; grandmothers or other relatives. So John Paul's insistence on women not being 'forced' to work – and this is his principal contribution to the discussion – derives from his need to object to the way things are done in Poland.

Comparable remarks can be made about birth control, abortion and divorce. Hennelowa tells the story of a primary school teacher who asked her class: 'How many of you have a brother?' A few hands went up. 'And how many have a sister?' More hands went up. But one girl had put her hand up both times. 'Why did you put your hand up twice?' asked the teacher. The girl replied: 'Because I have a brother *and* a sister.' Amazement. Everyone was dumbfounded. She came from an exceptional, eccentric three-child family. The official policy is 2 + 1 (which means that two parents plus one child is the norm) though 2 + 2 is tolerated. Hennelowa does not tell us how family size is limited, except to say that the number of abortions in Poland is 600,000 *per annum*, which is about the same as the number of live births. Divorce, she also reports, is running at 30 per cent in the big cities and 40 per cent in Warsaw.

So whatever else John Paul is doing when he condemns women being forced to go out to work, presents the mother as the heart of the home, denounces the evils of artificial birth control, abortion and divorce, he is not reflecting the Polish situation so much as reacting vigorously against it. Poland is not a model but a warning example of how things can go wrong. Our image of well-disciplined Catholics faithfully carrying out the orders of the hierarchy is a mirage. The 'secularization', which John Paul so often presents as a threat to the West, has eaten deep into Polish society.

An old book of moral theology had in its index under the entry 'Women': 'See *scandal* or *sex*.' However hard I have tried to keep sexual morality out of this chapter, it has edged its way ineluctably in. One begins with woman as archetype and ends up at the factory bench or the kitchen sink or the ironing board. Woman remains Eve.

11

Ethics and Sexuality

Fray Luis de León, lecturer in theology at Salamanca in the sixteenth century, returned to the classroom after several years in the prisons of the Holy Inquisition and coolly began his lecture: 'As I was saying yesterday . . .' In much the same spirit Pope John Paul II, on Wednesday, 11 November 1981, climbed the twelve steps up to his chair in Nervi's Mid-Atlantic Audience Hall, and said: 'Let us resume today, after rather a long break, the meditations begun some time ago devoted to thinking about a theology of the body' (11 November 1981). They had indeed begun a long time ago. It was more than two years before, on 5 September 1979, that John Paul had embarked on the vast and lengthy project which is nothing less than a treatise on the anthropology of the Book of Genesis, complete with learned footnotes.

John Paul has been criticized – from within the Roman Curia – for these Wednesday audiences. They are not instances of 'good communications'. In fact they are utterly mystifying for most of his hearers who by definition go only to one audience and do not know what has been said previously or what will come next. Visiting Japanese are puzzled at this display of Western religiosity. Pious Catholics have been known to blush at John Paul's frank speaking on sexuality. And even the brief summary in English which he reads out is difficult for those without a philosophical background. Here, for example, is what those attending the audience on 12 November 1980 heard:

We are continuing our reflections on the relationship

between *ethos* and *eros* in the context of Christ's Sermon on the Mount, in which he defines a lustful look as adultery committed in the heart.

From these reflections it is evident that the Christian *ethos* is linked with the discovery of a whole new order of values. According to these values, that which is erotic should be related to the meaning of the body in connection with marriage. If we do not make this connection, the very attraction of the senses and bodily passion remain at the level of concupiscence, and man does not experience the fullness of *eros* as a movement of the human spirit towards what is true and good and beautiful. It is indispensable that *eros* be reinforced by *ethos*.

These questions also touch the question of spontaneity. Sometimes it is asserted that ethical considerations remove spontaneity from the erotic area of human conduct. But those who accept the *ethos* proposed by Christ are still called to the full and mature spontaneity of the relationship that arises from the attraction of masculinity and femininity. This spontaneity is indeed the gradual fruit of the discernment of the impulses of one's heart.

Christ's words are demanding. They require that a person have a full and profound awareness of his own acts, and especially his interior acts, the internal impulses of his heart. There is an essential relationship between discernment and spontaneity. Christ's words contain the deep requirements for human spontaneity, which cannot exist in all the impulses that spring from mere carnal concupiscence. Deep and mature spontaneity comes only with self-control. (12 November 1980)

This is not the 'populist' Pope at all: it is the professorial side of Karol Wojtyla that comes out in these Wednesday audiences. And the reason he takes this approach is that he had a book drafted on this theme based on lectures delivered in Lublin University before he became Pope. As Pope, he cannot publish a book; as Pope, he must publish all his discourses.

When read as a whole rather than listened to one by one, the lectures make a good deal more sense. For the questions they raise are real questions – and very rarely faced. Few of us will ever have heard a sermon on the matter raised in the passage just quoted: does the introduction of moral norms into marriage lead to a loss of spontaneity in the sexual relationship? John Paul's answer is that it does not, and that self-control is a form of respect for the other in his or her difference. It is an illusion to suppose that where all rules are abolished and 'anything goes', the sexual relationship will be more satisfactory. But I do not want to stress this just yet. The more urgent question is to determine just what we are dealing with. What sort of discourse is this?

In these lectures (that is in effect what they are) John Paul is not behaving as a *moralist*, that is someone who enunciates particular moral norms and applies them to individual cases, but rather as an *ethical philosopher* concerned with the very foundations of morality and with the values that lie behind particular norms. Of course these two functions cannot be totally divorced from each other in practice. But they are distinct.

John Paul's starting point as an ethical philosopher is that 'the Christian *ethos* is linked with the discovery of a whole new order of values'. What are these values? What is specific about Christian morality? These are questions that have preoccupied Karol Wojtyla at least since 1954 when he first began to teach ethics at the Catholic University of Lublin. His second thesis (published in 1959) was called *An Assessment of the Possibility of a Christian Ethic based on the Principles of Max Scheler*. His conclusion was negative. Scheler had not succeeded in providing a valid foundation for Christian ethics. But the quest was on, and Scheler had at least provided him with a method of thinking, known as phenomenology, which he exploited in *The Acting Person* (first published in Polish in 1969).

130

Although not a treatise on moral philosophy, still less on moral theology, *The Acting Person* lays the foundations for Christian morality. It does what Scheler, according to Wojtyla, had failed to do. All the dimensions of the human person are taken into account: the person is responsible, responsive, embodied, sexed, intelligent, capable of free choices, of commitment, of acting 'with others'. He or she builds up his or her personality choice by choice, decision by decision, in the light of values and the perceived good. This is especially true of those basic commitments – say to marriage or religious life – which gather a life together, integrate its multiple aspects and 'make sense' of it.

In *Love and Responsibility* (Polish 1960, English 1981) Cardinal Wojtyla applied these principles to sexual ethics. The book grew out of a series of lectures given to Lublin students. It is therefore conditioned by this milieu. Most of his hearers were not yet married, and some were wondering whether they had a vocation to the priesthood or the religious life. Hence the chapter called 'The Rehabilitation of Chastity'. The book was the result, he tells us, 'of an incessant confrontation of doctrine with life' (p. 15), and he marvels that the New Testament basis for the Church's teaching on sexual morality should be found in a handful of texts (p. 16). The texts he mentions in 1960 are precisely those which he used as Pope to structure his Wednesday audience lectures. They are concerned with (1) an original state that was very different, (2) the fact of concupiscence, and (3) the resurrection of the body. We will examine these clusters of texts in a little more detail.

John Paul starts from Matthew 19:3–9 (and its parallels) which is concerned with adultery. It is this text ('Have you never read that the Creator made them from the beginning male and female?') that sends him back to the Book of Genesis, with the consequences we saw in the previous chapter. He has been greatly struck by Jesus's remark, 'It was not so in the beginning', concluding from this that there was a state of original innocence from which man (and woman) lapsed. As a result, 'shame' and 'concupiscence', hitherto unknown, entered into the relationship between men and women. And they are still present in so far as we are only inchoately redeemed and not yet fully healed. But God's intention is that male and female, through the discovery of what John Paul calls 'the nuptial meaning of the body', should be rescued from 'original solitude'. Male and female are destined for each other, for communion with each other, and in this way they become the image of God. Their communion results in procreation, which is a sharing in God's creativity.

The second key text is Matthew 5:27-32 which includes the verse: 'If a man looks at a woman with a lustful eye, he has already committed adultery with her in his heart' (5:28). John Paul's commentary on this passage in the Sermon on the Mount took a long time and was badly misunderstood. To give something of the flavour of his analysis, here is one of his English language summaries:

These words [Matthew 5:28] have a key meaning for us in understanding the whole theology of the body contained in the teachings of Christ. The correct understanding and interpretation of these words are important for us. They do not contain a condemnation or accusation against the body. Rather, they subject the heart to a critical examination. The judgement against lust which these words enunciate is an affirmation of the body, not a negation, as a Manichaean view would suppose.

The body in its masculinity and femininity is called, 'from the beginning', to be a manifestation of the spirit; this happens also through the conjugal union of a man and a woman. This kind of attitude has nothing in common with the Manichaean attitude, which negates the value of human sex or only tolerates it within the limits of the need for procreation.

Christ's words, instead, are the basis for a new Christian *ethos* which is marked by a transformation of people's attitudes. Through this transformation there is manifested and realized the value that the body and sex have in the original plan of the Creator, at the service of interpersonal communion. (22 October 1980)

No comment is needed.

The third panel of the triptych is the one that has so far been the least developed. It is concerned with the resurrection of the body and takes off from a discussion of Matthew 22:23–33, where Jesus is in controversy with the Sadducees. The key phrase comes towards the end: 'At the resurrection men and women do not marry, but are like angels in heaven' (22:30). Some astonishment was caused by the 2 December 1981 audience in which John Paul bluntly declared that marriage and procreation would have no part in eternal life. The beatific vision would be happiness enough. Peter Nichols conceded the perfect orthodoxy of this position, as well he might, but added: 'The question is being widely raised why he [the Pope] should have chosen to speak with such dogmatic assurance on a subject which modern opinion is inclined to leave on one side rather than to examine in detail' (*The Times*, 8 December 1981). But with the question comes the answer: in matters of sexual morality as in others, John Paul prefers the explicit to the merely implicit, the clear to the fuzzy, the risk of commitment to the ambiguity of embarrassed evasion. He follows the evangelical principle: 'Plain yes or no is all you need to say' (Matthew 5:37).

In his Wednesday audiences, then, John Paul has been setting down ideas that were already fixed in his mind in 1960. There has been no marked development. So although his formulations have a certain novelty for those unfamiliar with this style of thinking, and although he differs from his immediate predecessors in speaking more bluntly of 'the sexual urge' and unconscious impulses, the conclusions he arrives at are thoroughly traditional. The newish Jungian bottles contain old Thomistic wine.

His starting point, in *Love and Responsibility*, is a

distinction between 'loving' and 'using'. To 'use' someone is to reduce them to a means to an end. But 'anyone who treats a person as the means to an end does violence to the very essence of the other'. 'Loving', on the other hand, comes about when 'two different people consciously choose a common aim' and commit themselves to each other (p. 28). This simple distinction has ramifications in many directions. We have already seen its application to the world of work. The distinction explains why John Paul uses the words 'consumer' and 'consumerism' in such an unconventional way. For those schooled by Ralph Nader, 'consumerism' means being a wise and discriminating buyer. John Paul is closer to the Latin root, *consumere*, which means to 'use' or 'use up', to 'exploit'. So in his sense 'consumer' is always a pejorative term. The reduction of others to their mere 'usefulness' he sees as characteristic of capitalism and communism: both are instances of Utilitarianism. The moral horizon only begins to lighten where the other person is valued for his own sake and where the 'common good' is recognized as the goal.

Love and Responsibility has two prefaces by the author, one written for the Polish edition of 1960 and the other written in 1980 for the translations. They form an intriguing contrast and show that although John Paul's ideas have not changed in twenty years, his confidence in stating them has grown apace. In 1960 he still found it necessary to apologize for the intrusion of a cleric into this field. He replies to the argument that 'only those who live a conjugal life can pronounce on the subject of marriage' and that 'only those who have experienced it can pronounce on love between man and woman'. His reply is to concede a lack of 'first-hand' knowledge, but to assert a superior and much wider knowledge derived from 'pastoral experience'. One may well be sceptical about such a claim. It is extremely difficult and rare for married people to talk honestly, especially to a priest, about sexual problems; and other people's marriages tend to be impenetrable. But at least in 1960 Archbishop

Wojtyla tried to answer the objection that he did not know what he was talking about.

By 1980 he no longer bothers to apologize for his purely vicarious experience. Instead he asserts with great aplomb that his method was right and his conclusions were sound. For the book has gone on being written, he says, in the lives of those who put it into practice. Then comes this astonishing claim:

> This work is open to every echo of experience, from whatever quarter it comes, and it is at the same time an appeal to all to let experience, their own experience, make itself heard, to its full extent: in all its breadth and in all its depth . . . *Love and Responsibility*, with this sort of methodological basis, fears nothing and can fear nothing which can be legitimized by experience. Experience does not have to be afraid of experience. (p. 10)

Ever since the 'Modernist' crisis, the appeal to 'experience' had been treated with some suspicion by the *magisterium*, because it led to the peril of 'subjectivism'. So here we have one of the boldest and most revolutionary appeals to let experience count found in theological literature. (Ironically, the only contender in this field is Edward Schillebeeckx. He devotes thirty-five pages of *Christ*, SCM Press, London, 1980, to explaining that, anyway, there is no alternative to 'learning from experience'.)

The difficulty is, however, that one cannot predict what will happen in experience. Take one central proposition of *Love and Responsibility*. It is of great importance because it anticipates the conclusion, if not the argument, of *Humanae Vitae*. Archbishop Wojtyla maintained in 1960 that the use of artificial birth control involves one of the couple 'using' the other, reducing them to an object of sexual gratification, and so 'depersonalizing' them. He wrote: 'Sexual relations between a man and a woman in marriage have their full value as a union of persons only when they go with conscious acceptance of the possibility of parenthood' (p. 227). But Archbishop Wojtyla was on particularly thin ice here. For the married can reply that although what he says is very interesting, it does not correspond to their own experience. Indeed it might sometimes be the case that husbands who fall hungrily on their wives only during the 'safe period' are the ones who are really guilty of treating them as 'sexual objects'. Not that one can make a rule of that either. The appeal to experience in these matters does not immediately point to a single, verifiable and irrefutable conclusion.

At the 1980 Synod on the family the need for another look at the teaching of *Humanae Vitae* was inevitably raised. And those who raised it appealed, in a variety of ways, to the experience of the Christian faithful. So Cardinal Basil Hume spoke of those for whom 'natural methods of birth-control do not seem to be the only solution'. He added the significant remark:

> It cannot just be said that these persons have failed to overcome their human frailty and weakness. Indeed such persons are often good, conscientious and faithful sons and daughters of the Church. They just cannot accept that the use of artificial means of contraception in some circumstances is *intrinsice inhonestum*, as the latter has generally been understood. (29 September 1980)

Archbishop John J. Quinn, speaking in the name of the US Bishops, made a similar point. He quoted a Princeton study which showed that 76.5 per cent of American Catholic women used some method of contraception ruled out by *Humanae Vitae*. He noted that opposition to the encyclical was found 'even among those whose lives are otherwise outstanding in Christian dedication, and among theologians and pastors whose learning, faith and discretion are beyond doubt'. He was reluctant to dismiss all these people as characterized by 'obduracy, ignorance or bad will'. Nor could they simply be swept aside or ignored. He proposed, therefore, a post-synodal study group which would include 'both theologians who support the Church's teaching and those who do not'. It would go to work on the principle of Pope Leo XIII who had said that 'the Church has nothing to fear from the truth'.

Archbishop Quinn was promptly denounced on all sides. 'The sense of the faithful [*sensus fidelium*],' the German-language discussion group reported, 'is not discovered by counting heads but by consulting the *magisterium*.' And in his final reply to the Synod, John Paul enlarges on this point:

> The 'supernatural sense of faith', however, does not consist solely or necessarily in the consensus of the faithful. Following Christ, the Church seeks truth, which is not always the same as the majority position. She listens to conscience and not to power, and in this way she defends the poor and the down-trodden. (*Familiaris Consortio*, No. 5)

This is splendidly rousing stuff, but Archbishop Quinn need not feel perturbed. It answers a point that he never made. He did not think that the Princeton Report was the pathway to doctrinal truth. He presented it as part of the evidence that should not be ignored. But ignored it was, and John Paul's comment on the use of sociology was discouraging for the future:

> The Church values sociological and statistical research, when it proves helpful in understanding the historical context in which pastoral action has to be developed and when it leads to a better understanding of the truth. (ibid.)

That assumes that the truth is known in advance and that the only permitted role for sociology is to provide confirmation.

Cardinal Hume's proposals fared no better than Archbishop Quinn's. The final propositions of the Synod –

its official advice to the Pope – made no mention of conscientious dissent from *Humanae Vitae* or of the pastoral problems it raised. Cardinal Hume's request for an interpretation of *intrinsice inhonestum* (it has been translated in a variety of ways ranging from 'intrinsically evil' to 'not quite the best thing to do') went unanswered. But at least the Final Propositions did not speculate on the reasons why some might feel the need to use contraceptives. John Paul does not show a similar restraint. He offers a sketch of three types of contraceptive-user:

> Some ask themselves if it is a good thing to be alive or if it were better never to have been born; they doubt therefore if it is right to bring others into life when perhaps they will curse their existence in a cruel world with unforeseeable terrors.
>
> Others consider themselves to be the only ones for whom the advantages of technology are intended and they exclude others by imposing on them contraceptives or even worse means.
>
> Still others, imprisoned in a consumer mentality and whose sole concern is to bring about a continual growth of material goods, finish by ceasing to understand, and thus by refusing, the spiritual riches of new life. (*Familiaris Consortio*, No. 30)

These pen-portraits are John Paul's own work. Only the second category reflected the Synod: it got very worked up about third world countries having contraception or sterilization *forced* upon them. This was something that incurred universal disapproval.

It is difficult to resist the conclusion that John Paul knew in advance what the Synod ought to do, and that the members of the Synod knew it as well. They were not really there to 'inform and give advice' to the Pope, as the *motu proprio* which set it up said. For the Pope, an expert, did not need advice on this topic. So the function of the Synod changed. It became a celebration of the unity of the Bishops around the Pope in a reaffirmation of *Humanae Vitae*.

No one should have been surprised. For John Paul has always felt that *Humanae Vitae* (1968) vindicated his own thinking as developed in *Love and Responsibility* (1960). This explains his account of the aftermath of *Humanae Vitae* in the 1980 preface to his book. It is extremely revealing of his attitudes and his isolation from the debates that were going on in the rest of the Church. He distinguishes two phases after the encyclical.

In phase one there was 'a rather chaotic search for arguments and counter-arguments, as each side sought to win over supporters'. 'A chaotic search' suggests a rather hit-or-miss enterprise that is probably doomed to failure. However, these alarums are now long over, and the second phase is one of 'self-examination of a methodologically profounder kind' (p. 16). That this was the effect of *Humanae Vitae* is very debatable. The American Jesuit moral theologian, Richard A. McCormick, was more accurate when he summarized reactions to it as, in order, 'shock and/or solace, suspension, silence'. But John Paul does not agree. It is because he thinks that the *Humanae Vitae* debate has moved on to a profounder level that, at long last, the hour of his book, *Love and Responsibility*, has struck. And since he is Pope, he may well be right.

What he has to say on this subject – repeated on all his international journeys – is in essence very simple. 'One should not cheat with the doctrine of the Church,' he told one meeting, 'when it has been clearly expounded by the *magisterium*, by the Council, and by my predecessor Paul VI in his encyclical *Humanae Vitae*' (7 November 1979). Here Homer nodded: for the Council had nothing to say on artificial birth control, Paul VI having removed the topic from its agenda. But this speech – to a sympathetic group of French doctors, psychiatrists and marriage counsellors who have been working on a reliable alternative to artificial contraception – revealed a very pugnacious John Paul. There must be no concessions to 'so-called conscience', and 'so-called pastoral solutions' which bend the rules are intolerable. Then he went over to the offensive:

> It is good that married couples should grasp how this natural ethic corresponds to a properly understood anthropology, and in this way they will avoid the snares [*pièges*] of public opinion and permissive legislation, and even, as far as possible, contribute to the correction of public opinion. (7 December 1979)

On this occasion, he was speaking to the converted. He was applauded for his vigorous stand. It was reminiscent of the mood of the American 'Moral Majority'.

His apologists, should they chance to read this chapter, would doubtless say that it is 'obsessed with contraception and *Humanae Vitae*'. The reply is that I have simply followed the emphasis of the pontificate. If *Humanae Vitae* cannot be qualified by pastoral experience, then there is little profit in discussing the other questions which come up in the field of sexual morality: abortion, divorce, trial marriages, homosexuality and so on. Nor should this be taken to imply that if a concession is made on artificial contraception, then the whole package deal of promiscuity, abortion, homosexuality has to be accepted. They are all different questions. But at least the fact that John Paul and his apologists generally make such an assumption dispenses me from talking about these topics at all. Since there is a 'no' to artificial contraception, then *a fortiori* negative answers will be given to the even graver moral problems that arise.

Other Christians have quite different views on these and other matters. John Paul has deliberately asserted what he takes to be Catholic identity. So the question quite naturally comes up: how ecumenically-minded is John Paul II?

12

Talking with Other Christians

On the morning after he was elected Pope, John Paul II committed himself firmly to work for better relations between divided Christians:

> It does not seem possible that there should remain the drama of division among Christians, a cause of confusion, perhaps even of scandal. We intend, therefore, to proceed along the way happily begun, by favouring those steps which serve to remove obstacles. Hopefully, then, thanks to common effort, we might arrive finally at full communion. (17 October 1978)

This was what might be called the 'classic' case for ecumenism, as developed after the Council in the pontificate of Paul VI. It expressed the *motive* for engaging in ecumenical work (the scandal of divisions), hinted at the *method* to be followed (removing obstacles) and pointed unambiguously to the final goal ('full communion'). This was all less jejune than it might sound. For not everyone in the Roman Curia would accept that it was desirable to 'proceed along the way happily begun' – a phrase that was widely taken as approval of the dialogues already under way. Above all, the new Pope appeared to be looking to the future rather than to the past. And the commitment to ecumenism solemnly made on the morning after his election has been repeated on countless occasions since. This is what keeps the Secretariat for Christian Unity – the Vatican department responsible for contacts with other Christians – in business.

But there are other facts that are more disquieting. The

first is that a kind of schizophrenia has been introduced into much Catholic discourse. One kind of statement is made in an ecumenical context, while quite different statements are made, on the same topic, for internal consumption. The concept of 'ministry', for example, so painfully hammered out by the Anglican/Roman Catholic International Commission (ARCIC), left no mark at all on Pope John Paul's Maundy Thursday Letter to Priests (1979). As far as the Letter was concerned, the agreement might just as well not have existed. The Synod of the Netherlands Province of the Church (January 1980) and the Synod on the family later that year displayed not the slightest ecumenical concern. Both events were a celebration of restored and reasserted Catholic identity. Yet throughout that year, as throughout the pontificate, ecumenical language continued to be used.

What is the explanation of this marked discrepancy between the language used in ecumenical situations and the language used for Catholics only? I do not think that this schizophrenia should be put down to insincerity. John Paul means what he says about ecumenism. But he does not think, as his predecessor Paul VI sometimes did, that ecumenism is the central or most urgent task of his pontificate. Ecumenism is more a kind of postscript or afterthought rather than a dimension of everything else one does. The truth is that in Kraków John Paul had very little opportunity to engage in ecumenical work for lack of partners. The old law of ecumenism is constantly being verified: only those personally involved in the process of dialogue appear capable of profiting from the learning process which it entails. Those not so involved tend to misunderstand it and carry on as before.

It is not that John Paul does not know the theory of dialogue. In his Letter to the Presbyterian Church of Ireland, he notes that 'dialogue has been well described as a process of both making oneself understood and seeking to understand' (text in *The Tablet*, 15 March 1980, p. 275). But his own ecumenical encounters, crammed into the tight schedule of his international visits, were disappointing precisely because there was no time to 'seek to understand'. The Pope talked and everyone else had to be content to listen. Thus we have had monologues which are the negation of dialogue.

This was particularly galling in Ireland, where the Presbyterians were risking unpopularity in their own communities by the mere fact of going along to meet the Pope. Unable to talk with him, they had to be content with handing their prepared address to his secretary. It said that 'our ecumenical scene is at a standstill, if not in retreat'. They received a courteous reply, to which I will return, five months later. At Trinity College, Washington, on the last memorable day of the US journey, John Paul's address to the ecumenical gathering was notable for its emphasis on difficulties:

> Recognition must be given to the deep divisions which still exist over moral and ethical matters. The moral life and the life of faith are so deeply united that it is impossible to divide them. (7 October 1979)

That could be read simply as a useful and necessary plea for realism and a warning against being stampeded into unity. But it could also be seen as its indefinite postponement.

In ecumenical questions so much depends on emphasis, on nuances, sometimes on the positioning of an adjective. Given a choice between stressing what is held in common and what divides, ecumenists stress the former while John Paul tends to favour the latter. A typical example occurs in the apostolic letter, *Catechesi Tradendae*, which is his answer to the advice given (in fact to his predecessor) by the 1977 Synod on catechesis. After reminding Catholics that ecumenism is a duty imposed on them by Vatican II, and cautiously commending an ecumenical approach to catechesis, the text goes on:

> But the communion of faith between Catholics and other Christians is not complete and perfect, and in certain cases there are profound divergencies. Consequently this ecumenical collaboration is of its very nature limited; it must never mean a 'reduction' to a common minimum. (No. 33)

This is very grudging. It is unlikely to fire anyone with great enthusiasm for ecumenical catechesis. It is very different from the positive relish with which the English and Welsh Bishops say that 'Christians in their separation should do everything together except what conscience forces them to do apart' (*The Easter People*, St Paul Publications, 1980, No. 72). One senses that the Congregation for the Doctrine of Faith, the watchdog of orthodoxy, had a hand in shaping the Pope's views. The Congregation has 'specialists' in ecumenism who 'shadow' their counterparts in the Secretariat for Christian Unity. They are pulling in opposite directions.

The charge that ecumenism means a 'reduction to a common minimum' is frequently heard in the Congregation for the Doctrine of Faith. It crops up regularly in the pages of *L'Osservatore Romano* which talks readily of 'glossing over problems for the love of facile irenicism, and speaking the language of the separated brethren' (16 October 1981). Since no one is ever named, one does not know whether such comments are meant to refer to the ecumenical agreements that have already been reached, say with Anglicans and Lutherans. Certainly those engaged in these dialogues would strenuously deny that they were trying to 'reduce' Christian faith to a lowest common denominator. On the contrary, they imagined that they had complemented each other and found mutual enrichment.

The Anglican/Roman Catholic International Commission completed its work in September 1981. Its three agreed statements – on Ministry, the Eucharist and Authority, together with a final report answering objections and dealing with mixed marriages – have been presented to the respective 'authorities' who will have to make the next move. Canon William Purdy called the final report 'perhaps the major achievement of all bilateral dialogue since Vatican II' (in a lecture at the Foyer Unitas in Rome in November 1981). But who are the 'authorities'? On the Anglican side the answer is relatively straightforward: the agreements will be debated and reported upon by the twenty-seven Churches that make up the Anglican Communion. The curiously named Committee of Primates will have a co-ordinating role. The process will be lengthy and cumbersome. But that is the price one pays for having 'diffused authority'.

It ought to be easier for Catholics to say who their 'authorities' are. But it turns out to be a very complicated matter. Everyone emphasizes that it is not simply a matter of waiting for John Paul's personal response; for that would involve an exercise of the 'monarchical primacy' that would offend against the 'collegiality' advocated in the agreed statements themselves. Collegiality is the idea that the Bishops with the Pope are co-responsible for the whole Church. In this instance collegiality could be manifested by the Pope consulting local hierarchies and listening to what they have to say; and in such a consultation, the English and Welsh Bishops' Conference would naturally carry more weight than, say, the Polish Conference which knows nothing of Anglicans and has other, more pressing problems on its collective mind. For a brief time the idea was mooted that a Special Roman Synod should be summoned, composed of Bishops who were ecumenically competent or who had actual experience of Anglicans. But after the experience of the Dutch and Ukrainian Synods, where John Paul imposed his will, enthusiasm for this idea waned.

Thus, despite everyone's protestations to the contrary, what Pope John Paul personally thinks about these agreements matters greatly. What can we expect him to say on this topic when he comes to Britain? If he merely repeats what he has said before, the sense of disappointment and anti-climax will be great. In an address to the Plenary

Assembly of the Secretariat for Christian Unity he merely noted that ARCIC would complete its work the following year and added: 'The Catholic Church will then be able to pronounce officially and draw the consequences for the next stage' (8 February 1980). I cannot read this riddle even in the original French: *'L'Eglise catholique pourra alors prononcer officiellement et en tirer les conséquences pour l'étape qui devra suivre.'*

In September of the same year John Paul received the members of ARCIC and spoke in warmer and less enigmatic tones of their work. He referred to Archbishop Michael Ramsey and Pope Paul VI:

> As the two men who commissioned you realized deeply, oneness in faith lies at the root of Christian life and vivifies it. Given that, there can be a rich variety in growth. (4 September 1980)

But having placed ecumenism, correctly, on this spiritual level, he added that the relationship between the two Churches was still plagued by 'practical problems' such as the validity of Anglican orders (declared null and void in 1896), mixed marriages, inter-communion and 'Christian morality'. This list could be produced at any time to block progress.

However, the most important feature of the speech was the recognition that ARCIC's *method* had been fundamentally right. It was once described by Professor Henry Chadwick as a matter of getting beyond the sterile Maginot Line of past controversies in order to state what our common faith actually is today. John Paul described it in less picturesque but substantially identical language as

> going behind the habits of thought and expression born and nourished in enmity and controversy, to scrutinize together the great common treasure, to clothe it in a language at once traditional and expressive of the insights

of the age which no longer glories in strife but seeks to come together in listening to the quiet voice of the Spirit. (4 September 1980)

This was such an accurate statement of ARCIC's intentions that one suspected that the speech had been prepared in the Secretariat for Christian Unity. But John Paul read it out. So we must assume that he believes it. These ideas could provide a splendid theme for Canterbury Cathedral.

But once again there is a balancing qualification. John Paul's belated reply to the Presbyterians asserts a principle which, though it had a local application in Ireland, is obviously susceptible of a wider relevance:

> Inevitably such dialogue must first involve a small group of qualified representatives of either Church but, once they arrive at consensus, it remains difficult to translate words into actions until the results of the dialogue have been communicated to the members of the Churches at every level, often by a process which is itself a form of dialogue. (*The Tablet*, 15 March 1980, p. 275)

From one point of view this is sheer common sense. A dialogue 'above the heads' of the faithful would be difficult to implement. The 'experts' can reach an agreement that the 'men and women in the pew' take a long time to accept and assimilate. Moreover, John Paul is right to insist that *theological dialogue* is only one aspect of the ecumenical movement. The psychological barriers have to be broken down, the habit of living and praying together has to be established, and there is a long-haul pedagogical task to be undertaken. But on the other hand, such arguments, valid though they may be, should not be used as a pretext for delay. If we are to wait for the slowest ship in the convoy, it is unlikely ever to reach port. It would be sad if Peter's barque were responsible.

It was the visit to West Germany in November 1980 which

provided the stiffest test so far of John Paul's ecumenical credentials. First, it is the 'land of the Reformation' and the Lutheran Church has, for better or worse, helped to forge the national consciousness. Then the German Bishops ineptly put out a pamphlet which they had unwisely assigned to Professor Remigius Bäumer of Freiburg. He described Luther as a man 'whose uncontrollable anger and polemical spirit blinded him to Catholic truth'. His marriage to an ex-nun was described as 'sacrilegious and stained by fornication'. The papal condemnation of Luther was said to be 'inevitable' – a point that is disputed by many scholars today. So John Paul arrived in Germany with this unnecessary and embarrassing obstacle strapped to his back. The way he resolved the difficulty may provide a clue to his British visit, which has some comparable problems.

First there was an ecumenical prelude. The most northerly point of his journey was to Osnabrück where before the war Catholics were only 5 per cent of the population. Refugees and immigrant workers have pushed this figure up to 15 per cent, but Catholics are still in a minority. They are, said John Paul, in 'a diaspora situation'. It is an area where Catholics have good reason to be grateful to the Evangelicals who lent them churches until they could build their own. John Paul acknowledged all this:

> In the last decade the ecumenical movement has shown how close you are to your Evangelical brothers and how much you have in common with them when both you and they live honourably and coherently according to faith in our Lord Jesus Christ. (16 November 1980)

Did this mean that there were currently on offer dishonourable and incoherent versions of Christian faith? John Paul was not saying. He planted a niggling seed of doubt. But he showed himself to be strongly in favour of ecumenism, at least as a spiritual attitude. And in a splendid phrase he said that 'all ecumenical conversation, all joint prayer and action, are already enfolded in the prayer of Christ that "all may be one"' (ibid.).

But all this was a preliminary staking out of the ground. Those concerned about the 'next stage' of ecumenism were spiritually upstaged. The Evangelical Church leaders were worried about precise problems such as inter-marriage and inter-communion, and about the right to hold ecumenical services on Sundays (the German Catholic Bishops disliked Sunday ecumenical services because they stopped their people from going to Mass – one service was enough). They also regarded the papacy itself as a problematic institution. These were the thoughts in the minds of the nine EKD (*Evangelische Kirche Deutschlands*) leaders as they gathered in the chapter house of the diocesan museum in Mainz on 17 November 1980, at eight o'clock in the morning. Would John Paul descend from the ecumenical fence? Would he say something to offset the catastrophic image of Martin Luther presented in the pamphlet commissioned by the German Bishops?

Yet again John Paul revealed his talent for the unexpected. He simply shifted the ground of the question. His address was a commentary on the Epistle to the Romans which Luther had called 'the heart of the New Testament'. To everyone's astonishment, John Paul rehearsed most of the favourite Lutheran and Evangelical themes:

> We have all sinned. We cannot therefore judge one another. Jesus Christ is the salvation of us all. He is the one mediator. Through him the Father grants us pardon, justification, grace and eternal life. We must all confess these truths. (17 November 1980)

It was a remarkable performance. For a brief moment it seemed as though John Paul was on the verge of announcing that he had become a Lutheran. But it was not to be. He rescued himself at the last gasp with a quotation from Luther's 1516–17 Lectures on the Epistle to the Romans.

Luther was still in his Catholic phase, and he said that 'justifying faith involves not only faith in the person of Christ but faith in "what Christ is"'. John Paul took this to mean that faith in the person of Jesus could not be separated from faith in Jesus the founder of the Church; and therefore that to believe in Jesus is also to believe 'in the Church and its authentic preaching of the Gospel'. This move neatly set the early, Catholic Luther against the late, post-break Luther. The whole *raison d'être* of the Lutheran Church was abolished at a stroke. The Evangelicals did not know what to make of all this. They were nonplussed. They had arrived with a precise shopping list, but it would now seem petty-minded and churlish to go back to it after such a lofty exposition, in which most of their Lutheran clothes had been stolen.

It is true that afterwards the Lutherans declared themselves to be delighted. But what else could they say? They had got no for an answer. And they were reduced to congratulating themselves on the fact that the meeting with John Paul had overrun its schedule by ten minutes. Little did they know that for him, to be ten minutes late is practically to be punctual.

So far the discussion has been about dialogue with 'Western' Churches, with Churches that came into existence because of the Reformation. However, it must not be forgotten that the Vatican Council gave a special place to the Anglican Communion as one of those communions 'in which some Catholic traditions and institutions continue to exist' (*Unitatis Reintegratio*, No. 13). But it cannot be denied that John Paul's personal inclination is not to engage in dialogue with the Churches of the West, which he sees as corroded by secularization, but to turn rather to the Orthodox Churches which, in practice, are mostly within the Soviet Union's sphere of influence.

There are two reasons for this oriental preference, which is only disconcerting because of our ignorance. The first is that the long debate among Polish theologians in the 1970s, about the peculiar 'Polish contribution' to theology, was eventually resolved in 1978 by the suggestion that as Slavs brought up in the Latin tradition, they were particularly well-placed to interpret to the West the riches of the Orthodox tradition. There was a resolution in this sense at the 1978 Congress of the Polish Theological Association – the last to be attended by Cardinal Wojtyla. Hitherto, it had to be admitted, 'Polish theology' had been a euphemism for the rejection of Western (largely Dutch or German) theology. Now that the Poles had discovered a theological vocation, Cardinal Wojtyla eagerly endorsed it. This would be, he remarked, 'a sensible division of theological labour'. Two months later he was Pope, the attraction to the Orthodox was intensified, and good relations with the Orthodox were a necessary complement to his *Ostpolitik* generally. If Eastern Europe was to be brought back within the ambit of the 'wider Europe' of which he dreamed, then the Orthodox Churches had a vital role to play.

John Paul stated very clearly the second reason why relations with the Orthodox had priority, when he went to the Orthodox Cathedral of St George in Istanbul in November 1979. (It was during this visit that Mehemet Ali Agca announced that he would assassinate 'this Christian crusader'.) He said that unity between the Catholic and Orthodox Churches 'would be a fundamental and decisive step in the progress of the entire ecumenical movement. Our division has not been without influence on later divisions' (30 November 1979). Dialogue with the West is not being rejected here: but it is relegated to the second place because dialogue with the Orthodox is regarded as more fundamental.

The theory behind this far from self-evident position was elaborated by Yves-Marie Congar, OP, and others in the 1950s. If the schism between East and West had not occurred – it is conventionally if inaccurately dated 1054 – then the Reformation would have been unnecessary. The Roman Church would not have been able to impose its feudal and juridical pattern on the whole of the West. Belonging to one Church would not have been incompatible with a wide variety of traditions, customs and liturgies. Admittedly this is all rather speculative.

But it is certainly a thought that is uppermost in the mind of John Paul. In his speech to the Plenary Assembly of the Secretariat for Christian Unity, he made the priority of the Orthodox Churches in dialogue explicit:

> I am convinced that the rearticulation of the ancient traditions of East and West and the balanced exchange that would result from rediscovered full communion could be of the greatest importance for the healing of divisions born in the West in the sixteenth century. (8 February 1980)

There may, of course, be other reasons for the priority given to the Orthodox. It is among the Orthodox Churches that John Paul finds support for many of the positions he has taken up within the Roman Catholic Church: his insistence on 'high' christology, sacramental doctrine, mariological devotion, monasticism, a 'sacred' view of the priesthood, resistance to 'secularizing' trends and so on.

It is fair to say in conclusion that John Paul is not unecumenical, still less anti-ecumenical, but that he is ecumenical in his own way (*à sa manière*). But there is one particular question, already alluded to in this chapter, which requires special treatment: the papal office itself, if interpreted strictly according to the definitions of Vatican I, remains an insuperable obstacle to unity for the Anglicans, the Lutherans and the Orthodox and indeed for Christians generally. So it becomes imperative to ask what John Paul thinks about his own office, which Providence entrusted to him. That will be the subject of the next chapter.

13

The Papacy as Problem

Ecumenical dialogue, whether with the Orthodox, the Anglicans or the Lutherans, sooner or later stumbles upon the problem of the papacy. It can be 'put into brackets' for a time, while more promising lines of Christian convergence are pursued, but eventually it has to be faced. It seemed at first that John Paul had considered this question and had an interesting approach to it. On the day after his election he recalled the threefold scriptural foundation of his office as successor of St Peter: he is the 'rock apostle' (Matthew 16:18-19); he is commanded to 'confirm the brethren' (Luke 22:32); and to feed the sheep and lambs of the flock as a witness of love (John 21:15-17). He then went on:

> We are thoroughly convinced that all modern investigation into the 'Petrine ministry' must be based on these three hinges of the Gospel. What is proper and peculiar to it is becoming clearer day by day. We are dealing here with individual facets of the office which are connected with the very nature of the Church to preserve its internal unity and to guarantee its spiritual mission. This has been entrusted not only to Peter but to his legitimate successors. We are convinced also that this unique mission must always be done in love. Love is the source which nourishes and the climate in which one grows. (17 October 1978)

This was encouraging for ecumenists in a number of ways. The new Pope was agreeing that it was time to have another look at his office, and that scripture (and not the First Vatican Council?) would be decisive. The office would be redefined in terms of its purpose or function (rather than simply defended as an institution inherited from the past). And the emphasis is on love rather than jurisdiction. If this statement – which perhaps had been agreed before the conclave – did not quite indicate what would happen next, it was at least responsive to the ecumenical mood of the 1970s.

For many Christians had come to think that there could be 'a pope for all Christians' who would make visible the unity of the gathered Churches. But what was envisaged here was 'the Petrine ministry' rediscovered in its Gospel origins. Other Christians were prepared to accept that there was a role for the Petrine ministry, but on condition that it was 'reformed' and disengaged from the claims to 'infallibility' and 'universal jurisdiction' defined by Vatican I. There was an undeniable element of quid pro quo about this theory, though it was based not on feeble compromise but on a better understanding of the Gospel. The heirs of the Reformation had abandoned the view that the pope was anti-Christ and anti-Gospel; while the heirs of the Counter-Reformation were reminded that Vatican I was a 'time-conditioned' Council which used terms that could not simply be 'read back' into the Gospel.

So what was called for was an exercise in ecclesiastical and institutional humility. Some of the claims of Vatican I could be voluntarily waived. Authority, without ceasing to be authority, could limit its own exercise. 'I suspect,' wrote Raymond Brown, 'that the side which takes the first bold step will be recognizable as the most Christian' (*Crises facing the Church*, Darton, Longman and Todd, 1975, p. 83). Paul VI was aware of this problem, painfully, because he did not see what he could do about it. This is the meaning of his famous remark in 1967: 'The pope – as we all know – is undoubtedly the gravest obstacle in the path of ecumenism.' Paul VI had no intention of denying any of the claims made by Vatican I, and could not do so in conscience. But at the same time he had learned from his predecessor, John XXIII, that these claims did not have to be pressed, and that what counted in the eyes of the separated brethren was the *actual exercise* of the papacy.

By summoning a Council, John XXIII had shown that he did not regard his own office as the fount of all wisdom and initiative. He knew perfectly well that some Ultramontane theologians held that the definitions of Vatican I had made any further council unnecessary. Moreover, by insisting that the teachings that would emerge from Vatican II should not be declared 'infallible', he made the point that their acceptance would depend not on some supposed guarantee from outside but on their intrinsic and self-authenticating relevance. And far from being weakened in this way, the authority of the papacy was enhanced.

John Paul II presents us with something of a paradox. His popular success and evident friendliness towards other Christians would seem to fit him for the role of 'a pope for all Christians'. But apart from the 17 October 1978 statement, everything else he has said about the papal office suggests that he does not believe that it has anything to gain from voluntary self-limitation. On 15 May 1980 (released 22 May) he wrote a long and important letter to the German Bishops. Its main purpose was to thank them for the admirable way they had dealt with Hans Küng. But it soon became a mini-treatise on infallibility.

Küng had lost his right to teach 'as a Catholic theologian' on 15 December 1979. A hasty and improvised form of appeal confirmed the ban a few days later, on 30 December. Pope John Paul could have left the matter there. But with characteristic combativeness he wanted to join in the theological debate himself and offer an alternative view of infallibility to that provided by the incriminated Küng. This was a dangerous move. For it is an ordinary principle of interpretation even of a *doctrinal* text that it is the conclusions that matter; and any arguments adduced stand or fall on their own merits; they cannot gain in authority *as arguments* simply because they appear in a papal document. Since the letter to the German Bishops is not in any case an official text, there is even more reason for treating what he says with the respect one would accord to any other theologian.

The first question John Paul raises – and it is fundamental – is about the relationship of Vatican II to Vatican I. It was commonplace among theologians to say that Vatican II had *completed* the work of Vatican I which had been interrupted by war and the collapse of the Papal States. Because Vatican I only had time to talk about the pope, it presented a lopsided view of the Church which Vatican II would have to put right. To that extent the completion of Vatican I was also its correction.

But this is not how John Paul sees it:

> Vatican II inherited the teaching of Vatican I [on infallibility], confirmed it and set it in a new context, in the context of the mission of the Church which possesses a prophetic character because of its sharing in the mission of Christ.

All interpreters of Vatican II agree that it set infallibility in a 'new context', though they would describe the 'new context' differently. It had two principal features. First the pope was no longer seen in isolation as a lonely monarch set over the Church but rather along with the Bishops. They were *cum Petro* and not merely, as at Vatican I, *sub Petro*. The second novelty relative to Vatican I was that the *sensus fidei* (the 'instinct' of faith) and the *sensus fidelium* (what Newman called the 'con-spiracy of believers') were recognized as a theological source to which authority in the Church had somehow to be related. It seemed reasonable to suppose that these two principles, if observed, would gradually modify the exercise of papal authority. The papacy would become more 'collegial', more consultative.

We have already seen that John Paul reduces the *sensus fidelium* to insignificance (p. 137). He alludes to it in his letter to the German Bishops, but draws no conclusions from it:

In this context [i.e. the 'new context' of Vatican II] and in close connection with the 'sense of the faithful' in which all believers share, infallibility has the character of a gift or a service.

The same point was made, even more bluntly, in one of the Final Propositions of the Dutch Synod: 'The *sensus fidei* is not constitutive of revelation and has not the same value as the normative interpretation given by the *magisterium* of the Church' (No. 7). No sane theologian has ever contended that the *sensus fidei* is *constitutive* of revelation; they may have maintained that it is one of the instruments in its handing on But John Paul assigns it no positive role at all. There is nothing for the *sensus fidelium* to do. The old distinction, abolished by Vatican II, between the 'teaching Church' (*ecclesia docens*) and the 'learning Church' (*ecclesia discens*) is restored.

As for collegiality – the other factor for change – it has gradually been eroded. The Dutch Synod of January 1980 shows what it means in practice for John Paul. The Dutch Bishops were outvoted by the curial cardinals who attended the Synod on various pretexts. They were cut off from their people. They were invited to reject, point by point, what had been the basis of their pastoral policy for the previous fifteen years. Some canon lawyers have even cast doubt on the validity of the whole exercise. A synod should take place in the country concerned – not in a fifteenth-century room in the heart of the Vatican. In any case, it was evident that the Dutch Bishops had not been summoned to Rome so that the Pope might discover what they thought on certain important questions: they went to ratify the adhesion of their Church to the line of the present pontificate. *Sub Petro* prevailed over *cum Petro*.

Yet John Paul continues to speak the language of 'collegiality'. On every one of his international journeys it is the meeting with the local Bishops that is the most important. And John Paul invariably talks about the need for 'affective and effective collegiality'. For John Paul 'collegiality' means that the Bishops should back him up. This is not some idiosyncratic definition devised after he became Pope himself. In fairness it should be said that he has always thought in this way. At the 1969 'extraordinary' Synod – called to deal with the crisis of authority caused by *Humanae Vitae* the previous year – Cardinal Wojtyla explained that 'collegiality is a strong confirmation of the supreme authority in the Church, which belongs exclusively to the successor of St Peter' (*Karol Wojtyla e il Sinodo dei Vescovi*, Vatican Press, 1980, p. 162). No doubt. But is that *all* that collegiality means?

The fundamental point is this: John Paul does not appear to believe that Vatican II represents an advance on Vatican I. And in this way the principal argument for the reform of the papacy is removed. However, the advocates of repentance and reform had a fall-back argument based on the 'hierarchy of truths'. The decree *On Ecumenism* states that 'in Catholic teaching there is an order or hierarchy of truths, since they vary in their relationship with the foundation of Christian faith' (No. 11). This was addressed specifically to those taking part in ecumenical dialogue. Its intention, and its effect, were to release theologians from the obligation to take everything *en bloc*, to enable them to distinguish between essentials and accidentals, and to make Christ (the 'foundation of Christian faith') the supreme criterion.

Some theologians have concluded that papal infallibility has a low place in the hierarchy of truths. As Avery Dulles wrote: 'The life of the Catholic Christian is by no means centred on the papacy; it ought, at least, to be centred on God and Jesus Christ' (*The Resilient Church*, Gill and Macmillan, Dublin, 1978, p. 113). A further argument for a low place in the hierarchy of truths is the fact that the Church got along without any doctrine of papal infallibility for over a millennium. John Paul is aware of this objection and seeks to answer it in his letter to the German Bishops:

Although the truth about infallibility may rightly seem of less central importance and to have a relatively low place in the hierarchy of truths revealed by God and professed by the Church, it is, nevertheless, in a certain sense the key to the certainty with which faith is confessed and proclaimed, as also to the life and attitudes of the faithful. (*Bollettino*, 22 May 1980)

It would take a long time to unravel that sentence. At first he appears to make a concession to the critics ('may rightly seem'). But the second part of the sentence withdraws it. The metaphor changes: from 'hierarchy of truths' – which suggests elements more or less close to their vivifying centre – we move to the 'key'. Now infallibility becomes of the utmost importance, since in practice it is the condition of holding Christian faith with any certainty at all. That this is what John Paul really means is confirmed by his next sentence: 'When this essential basis of faith is weakened or destroyed, then immediately the most elementary truths of our faith begin to collapse' (Italian: *crollare*; German: *aufzulösen*). It would seem to follow from this that those Christians who have no doctrine of infallibility (and that means all except Catholics) can have no certainty in faith. That is hardly a very promising basis from which to engage in ecumenical activity.

John Paul's high regard for his own office came out most dramatically when an estimated 15,000 young people, inspired by Br Roger Schutz of Taizé, were crowded into St Peter's. (A year later, they came to London.) This was a great ecumenical occasion. Though Catholics were believed to be in the majority, there was no means of distinguishing between them and the numerous Protestants. For that reason it was a service of readings rather than a Eucharist, otherwise inter-communion, officially frowned upon, would have been rife.

Introducing John Paul, Br Roger summed up the work of a lifetime when he said: 'I have found my own Christian

159

identity by reconciling, in depth, the stream of faith derived from my Protestant origins and the faith of the Catholic Church.' So Schutz had come halfway and there he was in St Peter's, symbol of the Counter-Reformation, built on the sale of indulgences, joyfully acknowledging his double inheritance. The young people – some of them perched perilously on confessional boxes or clinging to pillars – applauded and waited expectantly for the Pope to speak.

They were rather disappointed. Not everyone could follow the six languages in which John Paul spoke. But there was no mistaking that the part of the address delivered in English was a lecture on the claims of the papacy. It was, in the context, an astonishing choice of theme, made even more astonishing by the manner in which it was presented. He began, naturally enough, with Peter:

> It was not to John, the great contemplative, nor to Paul, the incomparable theologian and preacher, that Christ gave the task of strengthening the other apostles, his brethren [cf. Luke 22:31–2], of feeding the lambs and the sheep [cf. John 21:15–17], but to Peter alone. (30 December 1980)

Even if we leave aside the exegetical difficulties raised by the two passages (the Lucan text, for example, seems to refer to a particular occasion and not to a general commissioning), there seems to be undue emphasis on Peter and a determination to separate him from the apostolic college. 'To Peter *alone*': he strengthens their faith, they have their faith strengthened.

'The charism of Peter,' went on John Paul, as though stating some self-evident truth, 'passed to his successors.' Then he reviewed the evidence from the first two centuries that the Church of Rome had 'played a leading role'. The list is familiar from apologetic treatises: St Clement of Alexandria intervenes to restore order in the church of Corinth; towards 110 Ignatius of Antioch greets the Church of Rome as one which 'presides over the universal assembly of love'; finally there is the famous epitaph of Abercius, dated about 180, and now in the Vatican museum. There the matter was left, tantalizingly vague. The link between the year 200, when the history lesson stopped, and the present, was left to the imagination of his hearers. The impression they were meant to take home was that 'the papal case' is securely based in scripture and tradition. There is such a case: but this simplified and apologetic presentation of it was inappropriate for an ecumenical occasion. It was as though John Paul was exploiting the occasion to score a point over the Protestants.

Finally we have to ask what kind of ecumenism can survive alongside this heavy emphasis on the papal role. It is characteristic of John Paul's ecumenism that he has little time for the discussion of difficult *theological* points. He prefers to think of ecumenism as a spiritual attitude which, in ways known only to the Holy Spirit, will bring about eventual unity. His favourite quotation from the decree *On Ecumenism* is the passage which says that 'conversion of the heart and holiness of life, together with prayer, are the soul of ecumenism' (No. 8). One cannot quarrel with that, without appearing deeply unspiritual. It does seem to postpone union indefinitely and it does not tell theologians what to do next. In *Lead, Kindly Light*, Newman wrote:

> I do not ask to see the distant scene,
> One step enough for me.

John Paul contemplates the distant scene, not the next step.

Examples of realized union are rare in Church history. 1980 was the fiftieth anniversary of the union between the Malankara Catholic Church of India and the Church of Rome. In a message to the Bishops of the Malankara Church John Paul said that the event they were celebrating was 'a characteristically spiritual event'. He went on:

Your spiritual fathers placed themselves by faith in contact with the Spirit of Jesus. They listened to him. They followed him. *Their unity with Rome was the result of their communion with the Spirit of Christ.* (Letter dated 1 December 1980, released 29 December 1980)

One hopes that this is not a model for the reconciliation with other Churches. In this case the Malankara Church consulted the Spirit, while the Church of Rome merely sat back and waited for the truth to dawn upon them. This 'return-to-Rome' attitude is not what Vatican II meant by ecumenism. It recognized that 'whatever is wrought by the Holy Spirit in the hearts of our separated brothers can contribute to our own edification' (*On Ecumenism*, No. 4).

Ordinary occasions are more revealing of underlying attitudes than the big, special occasion. At the start of the Octave of Prayer for Church Unity in 1981, John Paul attempted to present Pope Leo XIII as a pioneer of the ecumenical movement. Having mentioned the French abbé Paul Couturier, who started the Octave of Prayer, he went on:

Along with him, it is fair to remember with gratitude all those, whether Catholics or not, who promoted and encouraged these practices, often amid incomprehension. Above all one should mention my great predecessor, Leo XIII who, towards the end of 1895, recommended to Catholics a novena of prayer for unity during the period before Pentecost [*Provida Matris*]. (19 January 1981)

Since it was Leo XIII who, only a year later, declared Anglican orders to be 'absolutely null and utterly void' (*Apostolicae Curae*), he seems a somewhat unlikely patron for the contemporary ecumenical movement. And Anglicans could be forgiven for finding the reference to him, to say the least, untactful.

But John Paul is, in a sense, caught in a dilemma of his

own making. He does not wish to admit that Vatican II introduced any new attitudes into the Church, and therefore is reluctant to concede that Catholics were opposed to ecumenism before Vatican II. So he leaves out the most damaging bits of tradition (like *Mortalium Animos* of Pius XI in 1928 which poured scorn on the ecumenical movement and presented it as a trick of the Devil), and has recourse to the implausible device of claiming that Leo XIII anticipated future developments.

The theoretical answer to the problem thus created is easy: admit that the Church has learned something, gained new insights. The practical problem is more difficult to resolve: for it is undeniable that John Paul has an ecumenical attitude which differs from that which has been the basis of the work of the Secretariat for Christian Unity and its national commissions since the end of the Council. The ecumenical future depends upon how far John Paul follows his own instincts or how far he follows the advice of the Secretariat for Christian Unity.

14

The Shooting and After

At about 4.45 p.m. on the afternoon of 13 May 1981, Mehemet Ali Agca, who had slipped jail in Turkey and vowed to kill the Pope in November 1979, headed for the obelisk which stands at the centre of St Peter's Square. It used to be the *spina* in the circus of Gaius and Nero. If it could speak, it could tell us about the crucifixion of Peter of Galilee on a chilly October evening in the year AD 64. But Ali Agca was more interested in the present than the past. He asked a Benedictine monk, Dom Martino Siciliani, where the Pope would emerge from. He spoke in rather defective English. Siciliani, a seismologist from Perugia, did not really know the answer to the question, but anxious not to let the cloth down, he gestured towards the right and the 'Bronze Gate'. The young foreigner thanked him and moved off to the right. Shortly after five o'clock, Pope John Paul emerged from the opposite corner of the square. Siciliani felt mortified and foolish. He recognized his questioner later that evening when he saw the television playbacks. He reported this to the police.

Fr Siciliani's evidence was strangely neglected. It proved two important points. First, that the crime, though long premeditated in the strictest sense of the term, was not carefully planned in any detail. Ali Agca was ignorant about the most elementary features of a papal audience in summertime. Secondly, it confirms that he had no getaway scheme. Between the time he put his question to Fr Siciliani and the time he fired his Browning 9 at 5.19 he could not possibly have arranged for a car to be on hand in the crowded side-streets of the Borgo Pio. So perhaps he was telling the truth when he said that he worked alone and no longer wished to live.

The two bullets that he fired at 5.19 on that 13 May ought in all logic to have put an end to the pontificate. Ali Agca was a professional assassin who had already killed at least twice. He was shooting from a range of less than nine feet. Yet he did not kill the Pope. This was partly due to the courage of an intrepid nun from Bergamo, Sr Letizia, who chanced to be standing behind Ali Agca, realized what was happening, and pulled hard on his jacket, thus deflecting his aim. Afterwards an article in *L'Osservatore Romano*, written by the paper's deputy editor, Fr Virgilio Levi, sought to prove that since it was on 13 May 1917 that Our Lady had appeared to the peasant girls at Fatima in Portugal, it was Our Lady of Fatima who had providentially saved the life of the Pope. 'This is not the product of pious imagination,' he gravely added.

Fr Levi must have access to sources denied to ordinary historians. The plain fact is that on the evening of 13 May 1981, Pope John Paul came very close to death. He had lost much blood in the twenty-three-minute drive to the Gemelli Hospital. The colostomy operation began just after six o'clock and was not finished until 11.25 p.m. One bullet had penetrated the abdomen, while the other had struck the right forearm and injured the second finger of the left hand. The operation over, John Paul was by no means out of danger, for in such conditions of weakness there is always a risk of infection.

Thursday, Friday and Saturday passed with reassuring bulletins twice a day from the medical team of six. We do not know what John Paul's private thoughts were as he lay, his blinds closed, in the VIP room on the tenth floor of the Gemelli Policlinico. But his first broadcast words, spoken at noon on Vatican Radio the following Sunday and relayed by loudspeakers over St Peter's Square, were 'Praised be Jesus Christ'. These were the very words he had used on 16 October 1978, when he was presented to the people of Rome.

Then, with difficulty and in evident pain, he read out six sentences that will never be forgotten by those who heard them:

> Dear brothers and sisters, I know that in these days, and especially in this moment of the *Regina Coeli* [Queen of Heaven], you are united with me.
>
> I thank you for your prayers and bless you all.
>
> I am particularly close to the two people injured at the same time as me.
>
> I pray for the brother who attacked me, whom I have sincerely forgiven.
>
> United with Christ, the priest and victim, I offer my sufferings for the Church and the world.
>
> To you, Mary, I say again: *Totus tuus ego sum* – I am entirely yours. (17 May 1981)

It was as though the whole pontificate had suddenly been simplified, pared down to its essentials of forgiveness, prayer and praise. The vast crowds, the chanted slogans, the great religious spectaculars that had marked the first phase of John Paul's papal ministry were now over for the foreseeable future. But what did it all mean?

The question was, of course, unanswerable. But that did not prevent answers being essayed. Cardinal Ugo Poletti, Vicar of Rome who looks after the diocese of Rome on behalf of the Pope, found it incomprehensible. He told a candlelight meeting in St Peter's Square two days after the shooting: 'We make an act of reparation for this insane act which, directed against the sacred person of the Pope, is directed against the God whom he represents, and the humanity which he loves as a father.' Here the Pope appeared not merely as the 'Vicar of Christ', but as the Vicar of the Father. That was a novel theological view, attributable no doubt to the emotions of the moment. Most secular commentators reached for their clichés. They talked of 'outrage', 'indignation', 'dastardly crime'. They should have attended more to John Paul's words. Since the previous Easter Sunday his catechesis had been largely about the Good Shepherd who provides the 'pattern for the ministry' and who is ready to 'lay down his life for his flock'. He was ready to die. From his earliest philosophical studies he had always known that words and prayer are a form of commitment. Sooner or later they catch up with you. They have to be cashed. That is why on that Sunday, 17 May 1981, John Paul's words reached a level of 'authenticity' (to use another of his philosophical concepts) never before so limpidly attained. The pontificate that had been so frantic in pace and prodigal in words suddenly entered a new dimension. There was a pause for reflection, a moment of discernment.

Or so it seemed at the time. Most commentators were agreed that, whatever else happened, the assassination attempt would make some difference to the pontificate of John Paul II, at least in the sense of dividing it into 'before' and 'after'. Cardinal Basil Hume said:

> It is possible that a new kind of apostolate is now open to this ardent man. He has had his fill of mass meetings, and it could be said that the transient fervour of these occasions seems hardly relevant to the condition of humanity today. (Quoted in *The Tablet*, 1 August 1981)

Of course Cardinal Hume already had one eye on the visit to Britain, and he did not want the Pope's convalescent strength to be overtaxed.

Giancarlo Zizola, writing in the Italian weekly *Epoca*, claimed that there had already been a transformation of the papacy, and that it was reflected in the photographs that were appearing everywhere. Gone were the triumphalistic shots of the Pope as monarch greeting ecstatic crowds. Instead we saw a man evidently suffering, sharing in the human condition, propped up by pillows, surrounded by all the paraphernalia of modern medical science. He was the first pope to go to hospital; and the Gemelli Hospital serves Primavalle, one of the poorer and more chaotic suburbs of Rome. Zizola wrote:

> His throne is now a hospital bed. He governs and teaches from there. If the bullets of Mehemet Ali Agca had killed the Pope, then the Church would have had another martyr to honour on its altars, but nothing would have changed: the throne would have remained the throne. (*Epoca*, 17 June 1981)

But now everything had changed. The Church and the world look different when seen from a hospital bed. Zizola concluded: 'Those bullets did more to change the Church than a whole theological library.'

It cannot candidly be said that any of these judgements has stood the test of time. All of them made two assumptions which have turned out to be false. The first was that the convalescence would take a very long time – and that the Curia would fill the vacuum in the interim – and the second was that John Paul would be permanently weakened or slowed down if not actually incapacitated. Both assumptions were reasonable. Both were wrong. They went wrong because of John Paul's formidable resolution, his physical toughness, his refusal to admit defeat, and his sense of Providence. A year earlier in an interview with *L'Osservatore Romano*, he had said: 'Many people say the Pope is travelling too much and at too frequent intervals. Speaking from the human point of view, they are right. But it is Providence that guides me, and sometimes it suggests that we do certain things to excess' (13 June 1980).

With hindsight we can say that one of the excessive things he did was to emerge from the Gemelli Hospital too soon, and against the advice of his doctors (who, naturally, would never admit this publicly). The reason why John Paul wished to be released from hospital prematurely was perfectly evident. He did not want to miss the Feast of Pentecost which, in 1981, was not only the 'birthday of the Church' but was also the sixteen-hundredth anniversary of the First Council of Constantinople. John Paul saw this as an important ecumenical occasion that would evoke an event which preceded subsequent divisions by several centuries. On the vigil of the feast, Metropolitan Damaskinos of Tranoupolis, an Orthodox prelate, gave a 'meditation' in St Peter's: this had never happened before. The next day John Paul himself read out in Greek and in Latin the formulation of the Creed hammered out at Constantinople: it omits the word *filioque* ('and through the Son') which has been used in the West only since 810 when the Emperor Charlemagne imposed it on a reluctant Pope Leo III. Since the use of the term had been one of the grounds of controversy between East and West, the fact that the Pope omitted it was a sizeable olive branch.

John Paul's homily, however, had been pre-recorded, and he was not present at the Mass in St Peter's, which was presided over by Cardinal Carlo Confalonieri, the eighty-eight-year-old dean of the college of cardinals. Just before the blessing it was unexpectedly announced that the Pope would appear on the inner balcony of St Peter's. So those who were last were first. It was a dramatic moment. John Paul took a few steps forwards so that he could support himself on the balustrade. His white figure was framed against a sunlit window on the other side of the balcony. He waited for the applause to fade and then said, in a firm and resonant voice:

> Venerable brothers. I wanted to be present with you at the end of this eucharistic celebration today – yes, to be present with you in this basilica which has brought us together, just as the apostles were gathered in the upper room, 'with Mary his mother', to proclaim to the world 'the mighty works of God'. (7 June 1981)

It was a theme dear to John Paul: Mary at the heart of the praying Church. He had used it in the conclusion to

Redemptor Hominis. In this context, with the Pope just back from the edge of death, it was particularly moving.

But within two weeks John Paul had to be rushed back into hospital. A laconic bulletin explained that the Pope had been suffering from 'a slight but persistent fever'. He had gone into hospital for 'check-ups' (the English word was used) to determine its cause (20 June 1981). But only three days before the Vatican Press Office was maintaining that the Pope's condition was 'normal', that he continued to improve, that he was not vomiting and that his appetite was good. The Press Office's reputation for reliability was not enhanced. Journalists with no experience of medicine consulted doctor friends or medical encyclopaedias in an effort to interpret the symptoms. It became standard practice to hang around the foyer of the Gemelli Hospital in the hope of getting a comment from one of the doctors in charge of the Pope.

There were wild rumours and displays of ill-temper. It was reported, correctly, that Mrs Ann Odre, one of the women injured in the attack on the Pope, was also suffering from a mysterious, unexplained fever. This led to the hypothesis that Mehemet Ali Agca had used poisoned bullets. After all, he had spent a month in Bulgaria. Perhaps he had been trained there. Remarks made by Ali Agca on the day of the shooting now took on a more sinister meaning. Told that the Pope was going to live, he said: 'It's too early to say that.' When he heard that the two women had been hit, he said: 'I'm sorry for the women.'

The Polish nurses looking after the Pope also talked. They could not conceal their anxiety. One of them broke down and needed psychiatric counselling before she could resume. The terrible fear was that the first ever Polish Pope might die after too brief a pontificate. Other Poles, equally worried, tried to bring reassurance but in a not very helpful way. They gathered in St Peter's Square below the Pope's window and sang hymns around a copy of the icon of Our Lady of Czestochowa. They were trying to persuade 'their' Pope to appear at his window. They knew that John Paul would find this hard to resist. But what they did not know was that their satisfaction was the Pope's torment. It meant getting out of bed. It meant the laborious and painful process of dressing. On 17 June Archbishop Jacques Martin, Prefect of the Pontifical Household, went down into the Square and pleaded with a group of Poles to give the Pope some peace. Three days later John Paul was back in hospital.

The pre-recorded Angelus message of 21 June brought no consolation. John Paul now sounded weaker and more breathless than he had only two weeks after the shooting. The responses to the prayers indicated the presence of two men (the two private secretaries, Fr John Magee and Mgr Stanislaw Dziwisz) and, for the first time, a woman – one of the Polish nurses. It was the transferred Feast of Corpus Christi, and John Paul talked of the Eucharist as 'the pledge of immortality'. There was a note of leave-taking, of resignation that had never been heard before. The broadcast was so alarming that Vatican Radio, contrary to its usual practice, did not repeat it. This was certainly the darkest moment in the entire episode. The obituaries were brought up to date.

But within a few days there was a perceptible lightening of the mood. The 24 June medical bulletin was the most detailed to date. The heart, breathing and digestive systems of the patient were all working satisfactorily. The infection in the right lung – no doubt the reason why the voice sounded so breathy at the previous Angelus – had been dealt with. Radiological and ecographic investigations showed no evidence of pathological symptoms in the abdomen. Other tests indicated traces of a recent viral infection, but the 'cytomegalovirus' was benign. The bulletin did not estimate how long the convalescence would last, nor did it say when the second operation would be. That was routine professional caution. The important thing was that the virus was benign and that it had been named: in ceasing to be mysterious, it lost most of its power to alarm.

Thereafter John Paul's progress was steady. There were no further setbacks. Some of the doctors wanted him to go to Castelgandolfo in July so as to build up his strength for the removal of the colostomy. John Paul refused. He had been blamed for leaving hospital too soon the first time. This time he would stay in the Gemelli Hospital, even though feeling like a caged wolf, until he was better. On 19 July 1981 he was fit enough to do a forty-minute telecast for the Eucharistic Congress that was meeting in Lourdes. It was done in one take, though the heat was intense because the noisy air-conditioning had to be switched off. Since he was talking to people gathered at Lourdes, it was natural that he should make a brief reference to his illness: 'God has permitted that I too should feel, in my flesh, suffering and weakness. I invite you to offer with me your trials to the Lord, who realizes great things through the cross' (19 July 1981). This became, subsequently, his standard comment on the event.

He has never said anything – after the initial act of forgiveness – about Mehemet Ali Agca, or speculated about his possible motives or backers. Cardinal Agostino Casaroli, Secretary of State, was not so reticent. Deputizing for John Paul on the Feast of Sts Peter and Paul, 29 June, he implied that Ali Agca had not acted alone and that there had been a plot. That, at least, is what the following sentence was taken to mean: 'A hostile heart (or perhaps hearts) armed an enemy hand to strike at the Pope, and such a Pope!' This led to rumours of a KGB involvement. Meanwhile Ali Agca was tried, predictably found guilty and sentenced to life imprisonment (which, in Italy, means what it says). No evidence of conspiracy or plotting was produced at the trial. His defence lawyer, Pietro D'Ovidio, claimed that his motive was to become a hero for the Moslem world, someone whose name would go down in history. The cruellest punishment devised by the Italian prison authorities was to deprive Ali Agca of newspapers: he has never been allowed to read about his exploit.

So he would not have read the final medical bulletin – it

was the twenty-ninth – published on Thursday, 13 August, exactly three months to the day after his bullets had set the whole drama in motion. It said that the post-operative phase of the treatment was now mostly happily concluded, that Pope John Paul was free to leave the Gemelli Hospital, that he had been a most edifying and co-operative patient, and that a further six weeks' convalescence at Castelgandolfo would be needed. Then the team of eight doctors went off for their much-delayed summer holiday.

But John Paul did not leave the Gemelli Hospital on 13 August. As though to show he was master of the situation, he stayed on for another day, using the time to meet the children in whose 'community of suffering', as he put it, he had lived. The next day he left for the Vatican in his Mercedes marked SCV 1. It has a single armchair where the back seat usually is. John Paul's only concession to convalescence was to sit rather than stand, but he still managed to give his blessing and wave cheerfully to anyone he saw along the route.

His first act on arriving at the Vatican was to descend to the crypt of St Peter's to pray at the tombs of his three immediate predecessors, John XXIII, Paul VI and John Paul I. A Vatican spokesman solemnly explained that he was thanking St Peter for not having added to the number of tombs – for the time being. John Paul is ready to die, but not yet, for he has work to do. Providence has spared him *for a purpose*.

His first reappearance in public had been on the Feast of Pentecost. His second was on the eve and the Feast of the Assumption. This link with the liturgical year was not entirely fortuitous. It set his own experience in the framework of the mystery of Christ, Mary and the Church. John Paul was in buoyant mood on his return, and the atmosphere was relaxed and cheerful – 42 per cent of Romans were said to be away at the beach or in the hills. 'Rome is deserted,' said John Paul adding, not without satisfaction, 'but St Peter's Square is full.' The jokey mood continued. 'You may think I'm sweating,' he said in an improvised aside, 'but this has nothing to do with illness. It is because of the August sun.' He made a serious point about Poland. The Feast of the Assumption of Our Lady is a great celebration in Poland, where it is regarded as a kind of harvest festival, 'the feast of maturity'. A year ago, he said, the Polish people took a step towards maturity. He was referring to Solidarity.

John Paul docilely stayed at Castelgandolfo until the beginning of October, gradually increasing his daily work-load and the number of audiences. On Sunday, 25 October 1981, he consciously 'picked up where he had left off' by visiting the Rome parish of Jesus, the Divine Worker; he had been due to go there on 24 May, shortly after the Feast of St Joseph the Worker. He met all the parish groups, as usual, and his programme was no less strenuous than it would have been before the shooting.

Everything conspired to give the impression that the attempted assassination and its aftermath had been merely an *interlude* that was now definitively over. The Wednesday audience talks on sex were resumed. *Laborem exercens*, his first social encyclical, and *Familiaris Consortio*, his response to the 1980 Synod, were completed and published. The Jesuits were provided for. Plans for journeys to Nigeria, Switzerland and Britain went ahead. It was business as usual.

So the notion that there is a 'new model' John Paul, miraculously transformed by his sad and painful experience, is a fallacy based on wishful thinking. He has returned, if anything, with his previous opinions confirmed, and an even greater sense of urgency in communicating them to the rest of the Church. And he has the added authority of someone who has looked into the abyss of death. He has 'aged', of course: but that is a subjective judgement. And he has 'slowed down': but only in comparison with the truly vertiginous tempo he imposed on himself before the shooting. The English, Welsh and Scottish Bishops will have to be nimble-footed to keep up with him this summer.

Visitor to Britain

The thirty-seventh version of the programme for the papal visit to Britain is as follows:

Day 1 (Friday, 28 May). A.m. Arrive at Gatwick Airport. Mass at Westminster Cathedral, with all the Bishops of England and Wales concelebrating. P.m. Service for people who are sick, handicapped, disabled and dying at St George's Cathedral, Southwark.

Day 2 (Saturday, 29 May). A.m. Address to religious brothers and sisters at Westminster Cathedral. Then to Canterbury for a service at Canterbury Cathedral. Private meeting at Canterbury with leaders of other Christian Churches. P.m. Mass at Wembley Stadium.

Day 3 (Pentecost Sunday, 30 May). A.m. Open-air Mass at Coventry Airport. P.m. to Liverpool. At Speke Airport, the handicapped and other groups will be represented. Drive into city centre, calling at Anglican Cathedral. Service at RC Cathedral.

Day 4 (Monday, 31 May). A.m. to Manchester. Open-air Mass at Heaton Park. P.m. to York. 'Event' at Knavesmire Racecourse. Then to Scotland. The Scottish Bishops will make their own proposals for this evening and Day 5.

Day 6 (Wednesday, 2 June). A.m. Open-air Mass at Pontcanna Fields, Cardiff, for the people of Wales. P.m. Youth event at Ninian Park, Cardiff. (This will be for young people from the whole of England and Wales.) Then return to Rome.

There is no guarantee that this programme will be followed to the letter. But that was how it stood on 25 November 1981.

Every papal visit is original: one does not know in advance what John Paul will do or say. But at the same time the visits have conformed to a broad pattern. There are certain constants, and a few predictions, based on previous form, may be risked. But in this particular case there are two variables that could alter the regular pattern.

The first variable is that we do not know how much influence the English, Welsh and Scottish Bishops will have on the preparation of John Paul's sermons and addresses. At the time of writing, we do not even know who has been assigned the task of briefing him. He will be easily identifiable as the Bishop the Pope greets most effusively on arrival at Gatwick – because he will be the one he has seen most of most recently. In Ireland Bishop Cahal Daly helped; in the USA Bishop Thomas Kelly, OP; and in the Philippines Bishop Leonardo Lagazpi, OP. But all of them agree that their main function was to provide background information and the social and political context. They did not contribute in a major way to the content of what was said. For that, the Pope is his own man, and he will be insensitive to the argument, 'But you cannot put it that way in England'. 'Why not?' is his answer to that.

The second variable is that, despite everything that was said in the previous chapter, the long-term effects of the bullets of Mehemet Ali Agca are still not fully known. Certainly John Paul will not change his populist style merely because Cardinal Basil Hume finds it superficial. He might have to modify it in some respects if his old bouncing energy does not return and because security has now been made more stringent. No Bishops want to have another attempt on the Pope's life in their territory.

To give shape to this final chapter, I propose to ask four simple questions. To whom is the visit being paid? What will determine the main themes of John Paul's homilies? What may be expected on the ecumenical front? And finally, what is the visit really for, what is its hidden agenda?

To whom is the visit being paid? It sounds like an easy question. But ponder the words of HM Queen Elizabeth II during her state visit to the Vatican on 17 October 1980. Replying to the Pope's address of welcome, she rapidly surveyed previous royal visits to the Vatican, starting with Edward VII who met Leo XIII in 1903. Manifestly the Queen could not omit to mention the forthcoming visit to Britain, which had already been announced, but she spoke about it in a rather surprising way: 'Your Holiness will be coming to visit my Roman Catholic subjects.' This sentence was plainly false. His Holiness is not coming just to meet her Roman Catholic subjects; for one thing he is going to Canterbury to meet the Archbishop and to confer with other Church leaders, who are also her subjects.

Why, then, this misleading expression? I suggest two reasons. When asked about the nature of his visits round the world, John Paul has invariably described them as 'pastoral'. Now 'pastoral' is one of those over-used and broken-backed words that can mean practically anything. But in John Paul's thesaurus 'pastoral' means 'non-political'. Positively it means that his visits are directed *in the first place* towards Catholics for whom he has some kind of overall pastoral care. And it would be presumptuous and improper to behave 'pastorally' towards the rest of the community in Britain. This is what the Queen, or her aides, may have had in mind as they drafted this odd sentence.

They were also trying to say something else. The Pope's visit to Britain will not be a State Visit. Most of his other visits have been State Visits, and they have been governed by strict protocol. The Pope is treated as a head of state, which he is, and given a twenty-one-gun salute; he then has to inspect the Guard of Honour and listen to his own particularly lugubrious national anthem (the music is by Gounod, and there are no words); finally he rides in an open car or carriage with his fellow head of state. Presidents

Mobutu of Zaire and Houphouet Boigny of the Ivory Coast both cashed in on the papal visit to Africa and were seen as often as possible in company with the Pope. Both of them, incidentally, married the women they had been living with shortly before the Pope's arrival. (Asked about this, John Paul said: 'Let us say that this was the first fruit of my pastoral visit to Africa.') Even the establishment of full diplomatic relations with the Holy See, announced to Paisleyite growlings on 16 January 1982, did not change the nature of the visit. It was now described as 'the private visit of a foreign head of state'. In fact both the Foreign Office and the Apostolic Delegate, now Pro-Nuncio, claimed that the change merely 'cleared up an anomaly' and 'made no difference at all'.

But we can ask the question, 'To whom is the visit being paid?', in another sense. All his visits have been to *peoples* and to *nations*. He has a strong, quasi-mystical sense of the nation which he derives from his Polish experience, as we have seen. Each nation has its own destiny and story, its history, by which it is defined and given identity. This could cause problems when he comes to Britain. For he is coming to one state, the United Kingdom, but to three nations, England, Wales and Scotland. We already know that some Scots feel resentful at being tacked on as an afterthought at the end of the English visit, and there have been objections to the ingenious Union Jack logo.

If John Paul develops his usual themes on the importance of the nation in Wales and Scotland, he can hardly do so without giving support to nationalist or separatist feelings. It is likely that in both countries he will be unable to resist an analogy with the Tatras Mountains in Poland and say that he feels thoroughly at home in 'this beautiful land of mountains, lakes and song'. Even supposing this psychological problem somehow resolved, there still remains the other component in British Catholicism: the Irish. Ireland has already had a spectacular visit of its own, but it would be unjust not to recognize what Irish Catholics have contributed to Catholicism here. John Paul will have to remember this as he addresses himself to 'the English nation'.

But let us concentrate on 'the English nation' for, sentiment apart, that is what will count most for John Paul. The strange thing is that he has never set foot here before and has no first-hand knowledge of the country at all. Long before he went as Pope to France and Germany he had a very good grasp on their language and culture, and he had visited them repeatedly. It seems odd that he never came here, especially since the main purpose of his pre-papal travels was to visit Poles abroad and bring them a sense of *Polonia* – the wider Poland of which Our Lady is sovereign and Queen. Why did he never come to visit the 200,000 Poles in Britain? There may well be a political reason for not coming to London. It was associated with the wartime government in exile, and indeed a Polish 'cabinet in exile' still gloomily meets in Belgravia. Moreover, the Anglicized Poles were tenacious anti-communists and made a significant contribution to counter-espionage. But whatever the reason, the fact that he did not come means that he will arrive innocent of any direct knowledge of the country. There is one 'British subject' whom he sees daily – his English-language secretary, Fr John Magee – but he is an Ulsterman.

Nor is there any evidence of wide reading to make up for this absence of direct experience. In his philosophical work, *The Acting Person*, the dominant influences are German (Edmund Husserl and Max Scheler) or French (Paul Ricoeur). Only four English philosophers even rate a mention in what is otherwise a very large and comprehensive book. They are Jeremy Bentham, John Stuart Mill, A. J. Ayer and R. M. Hare. John Paul has constantly denounced the first two for their 'utilitarianism'. Ayer and Hare are merely mentioned in a footnote as purveyors of 'emotivism' and 'prescriptivism' respectively. Neither term is explained. Both philosophers are, however, summarily dispatched. In the whole vast output of the pontificate, I have discovered one quotation from John Henry Newman, but since it came in a letter to the Rector of the English College, it was doubtless put there by the Rector himself. John Paul, then, is coming to an unfamiliar country with an unfamiliar culture.

Detailed briefing can help to remedy these lacunae. But one thing is reasonably certain: John Paul will bring to the consideration of the facts laid before him a certain *image* of England that will tie all the disparate details together. This is another consequence of his habit of giving the *nation* an identity and a role in history. Of course it works better for 'Catholic' nations. In Brazil he linked the birth of the nation to the first Mass said there on the Feast of the Holy Cross in 1500. In the Philippines he said Mass in Cebu City, cradle of Catholicism in the East, where Ferdinand Magellan planted a cross in 1521. As we have seen, in Germany he talked about St Boniface who evangelized the country. This is all based on the analogy of Poland, where the baptism of the King in 966 was regarded as the birth of the nation. John Paul always tries to return to the origins, the *founding act* which establishes, simultaneously, Christianity and the nation. And this idea of an original, founding act, by which Christ breaks into the history of a given people, is not just a matter of more or less accurate historical reminiscence. On the contrary, from the founding act a national vocation flows. Thus in Brazil, John Paul suggested that its vocation was to integrate the most diverse races, while the role of the Philippines is to act as the missionary centre for the whole of Asia. What vocation will be assigned to England, Our Lady's Dowry?

One cannot say. What is certain is that we shall undoubtedly hear a great deal about our own *founding act*. In 597 St Gregory the Great sent Augustine and forty monks to England. On the following Christmas Day they are said to have baptized 10,000 souls in Canterbury. One hopes that John Paul's advisers will have read Jeffrey Richards's book, *Consul of God, the Life and Times of*

Gregory the Great (Routledge and Kegan Paul, 1980). He makes three points about Augustine's mission that are worth noting. Gregory's motive in sending Augustine to Britain was that he believed the end of the world was nigh: this gave added urgency to the mission. As he went through Gaul, Augustine heard such alarming reports about the ferocious bloodthirstiness of the islanders that he wanted to turn back: Gregory ordered him to press on. The reason Augustine and his monks could have such a spectacular baptismal success on Christmas Day was that the Gaulish Queen and her chaplain had already prepared the ground.

So we have our founding act. It is not too difficult to establish, and it sets up a direct link with the Holy See, the pope. The difficulty will lie in deriving a vocation for the English nation from this founding act. For at the Reformation – in the Pope's eyes – England lost its way and its vocation. Subsequently it knew power and the glory of Empire – precisely at the time when Poland was battered into non-existence as a state – but now it has been brought cruelly low. From the outside we look like a cantankerous, divided, violent off-shore island of Europe that, having exploited the third world, is still living above its means. Sometimes it is salutary to see ourselves as others see us. Max Scheler, on whom Karol Wojtyla wrote his second thesis, was a philosopher, but during the First World War he wrote propaganda pamphlets for the German government. As a Catholic convert (twice) he maintained that the Central Powers, Germany and Austria-Hungary, were waging a campaign for *Christian civilization* against a coalition made up of the godless French, who had disestablished the Church and driven out the religious orders in 1904, the Protestant English who were notoriously a nation of shopkeepers, and the truly frightful autocracy of the Russian Czars, who were supported and fawned upon by an effete and subservient Orthodox Church. Ranged against that you had Bach and Beethoven and Kant. John Paul's father would have been subjected to that kind of propaganda, and he would certainly have appreciated the point about the autocracy of the Russian Czars. I do not say that John Paul thinks such thoughts. But every time he denounces 'consumerism' and 'utilitarianism', there is an echo of Scheler denouncing the English as shopkeepers. And leaving aside the First World War, I have yet to meet a Pole who, while grateful for our well-meaning support in 1939, does not deplore the fact that at Yalta Poland was in effect surrendered to Stalin, without even a whimper of protest. General Jaruzelski's imposition of martial law on 13 December 1981 rubbed salt in that old war wound.

All this will somehow enter into John Paul's *image* of England. No doubt he will keep his feelings in check. An equally grave problem is that English national consciousness, as a result of history, is very largely shaped by the Reformation. John Paul faced the same problem in Germany, where he resolved it by inventing a 'German tradition' that was almost wholly Catholic. He could do the same thing in England. Unless the English Bishops manage to stop it, we could have a *1066 and All That* version of our history in which the main figures are St Augustine of Canterbury, St Edward the Confessor, possibly King Canute, St Thomas Becket (with a parallel with St Stanislaw of Kraków, his near contemporary), St Thomas More ('died for the papacy'), Bishop Challoner ('simple piety and rugged common sense'), Cardinal Manning ('friend of the dockers') and Cardinal Newman ('saw the light').

The second question is: what will be the main themes of the homilies? All the precedents suggest that they will be determined either by the category that John Paul thinks he is speaking to, or by the setting.

John Paul thinks in categories. For him an ideal visit would include meetings with workers, farmers or peasants, students, young people, intellectuals, artists, media people, priests, religious men, religious women. It worked during the visit to Poland. It is unlikely to work here. The fact that the Bishops have decided on a visit to each of the five provinces rules out for the most part meetings by categories. In each place there will be a general congregation of local people. However, there are two categories he is certain to meet separately: the Poles and the sick; and the final meeting of the journey, at Ninian Park in Cardiff, is for young people.

If then, on the whole, the content of the homilies will not be determined by categories, the alternative is to let the setting suggest the theme. This was seen supremely in Poland, particularly in Victory Square. But the same sense of history added wings to his words outside the Cathedral of Notre Dame in Paris: he was close to where Aquinas taught and where the tumbrils of the Revolution rolled. Even in the United States, he was able to draw on historical memories: the Liberty Bell in Philadelphia, and at Battery Park in New York, within sight of the Statue of Liberty, he was close to Ellis Island where so many immigrants began their American dream.

In comparison Coventry airport, Wembley Stadium, Heaton Park, Manchester and the Knavesmire Racecourse, York, do not offer quite the same scope for historical memories. Even so the context will probably determine the content of the homilies. Coventry will provide an opportunity to speak about reconciliation between nations and also, no doubt, about unemployment. In *Laborem exercens* he wrote that unemployment 'is in all cases an evil and, when it reaches a certain level, can become a real social disaster' (No. 18). With over three million unemployed, have we reached that 'certain level'? Liverpool would be an appropriate place for a homily on race relations, as the first anniversary of the Toxteth riots approaches. The heroism of the English Martyrs could be recalled in York where St Margaret Clitheroe was crushed to death.

Historical memories will be unleashed most obviously in Canterbury. I have already mentioned Canterbury in connection with the founding act that establishes the vocation of the English. John Paul will go there and make an ecumenical 'gesture'. By 'gesture' I do not mean empty display but rather a 'sign', a lived parable. This is something that we have learned from the Orthodox. For example the kiss of peace exchanged between John Paul and Demetrios I, the Ecumenical Patriarch, in Constantinople in November 1979 signified that the two Churches considered themselves as 'sister Churches'. It also implied some sort of equality and therefore a scaling down of Roman claims. No doubt Dr Robert Runcie and Pope John Paul will exchange a kiss of peace, thus confirming what Paul VI said about 'sister Churches' when he canonized the Forty English and Welsh Martyrs on 25 October 1970.

But John Paul will also have to say something. What that will be will depend on how the balance works out between the promptings of the Secretariat for Christian Unity and John Paul's conscience and sense of the dramatic. It is clearly too soon for him to declare official approval of the work of ARCIC, but he can at least thank the members of the Commission and wish its successor, popularly known as Ben-ARCIC or Son-of-ARCIC, well. Some ecumenists hope that John Paul will take a positive view of mixed marriages, regarding them as 'inter-Church' marriages and an antici-pation of the future reunion of the Churches. Others hope (while yet others dread) that he will announce a reopening of the question of Anglican orders. The theology of the ministry has moved on in both Churches since 1896 and, in the opinion of most theologians, converged. But neither on mixed marriages nor ministry has John Paul said anything in the past to suggest that he is ready to budge from the most rigorous positions.

One suggestion that has been much canvassed is that John Paul might give a pledge that in any future union the Anglican Communion would have 'Uniate' status. This means that its autonomy and its traditions – such as forms of worship and married priests – would be fully and not grudgingly accepted as the Anglican contribution to the enrichment of the Catholic Church as a whole. Dr Runcie has in effect asked for such a pledge in an interview in *The*

Universe. The reason why it would have to be guaranteed in advance is that the Vatican has not always been accommodating towards Uniate Churches. So for example they have not been allowed to follow their tradition of married priests when not on their own territory, on the grounds that this would upset the celibate Latin rite priests. One can understand why the Anglican Communion would be chary about Uniate status, unless it were accompanied by reliable guarantees against the erosion of its rights.

The Canterbury meeting is the most open-ended and unpredictable of the entire visit. John Paul could choose to evoke the 'new' difficulties that have arisen in recent years – the ordination of women and theological scepticism (what has been called *The Myth of God Incarnate* syndrome). Or he could stress a vague and spiritual unity, placed inaccessibly far in the future. Or he could spring a surprise. Just as in Germany he offered a 'Catholic' version of Martin Luther's thinking, he could reread the Anglican divines of the seventeenth century and show (and it can be done) just how deeply 'Catholic' they were.

That brings us to our final question. What is the point of this visit? Has it got a hidden agenda? All the other visits of John Paul have had a precise purpose: to deal with what he sees as the outstanding problems or weaknesses of the local Church. And the occasion for this is invariably the meeting he has with the local Bishops – the one meeting that is never televised and to which press and public are never admitted. In Chicago the US Bishops were told to hold the line on contraception, abortion, homosexuality and divorce. It was not, of course, being suggested that they had been advocating such evils, but that in the name of 'false compassion' or 'a pastoral approach' they had not displayed enough zeal in denouncing them. In Kinshasa, Zaire, the Bishops were warned about excessive and hasty 'Africanization' of theology and worship. The French Bishops were told that with a little more resolution they could roll back the incoming tide of secularization, and they were urged to supervise theological journals with greater vigilance. The German Bishops were exhorted to preach the unadulterated Word of God, without bothering whether it brought them plaudits or brickbats. The pattern is constant. There is no reason to suppose that the visit to Britain will depart from it.

Indeed the visit was first decided upon in August 1980 when Cardinal Hume and Archbishop Derek Worlock went to present to John Paul the documents of the National Pastoral Congress and *The Easter People*, the Bishops' official response to them. The whole event generated a great deal of excitement and enthusiasm and a sense of a fresh dawn breaking for English Catholics who, at last, emerged from the ghetto and advanced towards a new maturity, confident, committed, hopeful, and ready to play a part in English society. 'We all sensed,' said Cardinal Hume in his final words to the Congress, 'the presence of the Holy Spirit, and in a quite remarkable way.'

But what John Paul sees in these documents is something quite different. He finds a reopening of a whole Pandora's box of questions which he considers closed. He can read, for example, the suggestion that 'careful consideration should be given to the question of whether it be God's will that married men should at this time be called to the priesthood' (*The Easter People*, No. 95). He learns that some had proposed that the ordination of women should be 'explored seriously at this time' (No. 96). Even though the Bishops observe that it was inopportune to raise this question in Rome, they do not show the energy in rejecting it that is expected of them. The National Pastoral Congress also asked for 'further reflections on responsible parenthood and the moral problems which contraception poses for the Catholic conscience' (No. 103). No one could seriously believe that the 1980 Synod on the family satisfied this demand for 'further reflection'.

So the purpose of the visit is to recover the ground deemed to have been lost in Liverpool. It was not simply that the

National Pastoral Congress uttered dangerous opinions and that the Bishops were feeble in not repudiating them. There is the further consideration that the National Pastoral Congress was an instance of a kind of 'democracy' in the Church, at least in the sense that what the laity said was listened to and taken seriously by the Bishops. Here is an example of this listening and learning. At the Synod of 1980, a few months after the National Pastoral Congress, Archbishop Worlock argued eloquently that people in second marriages might in some circumstances be readmitted to the sacraments. He answered the inevitable objection that such compassion would be a scandal to the faithful and a blow to the indissolubility of marriage by an appeal to the experience of the National Pastoral Congress: 'Those who most vigorously uphold the Church's teaching on indissolubility, also ask for mercy and compassion for the repentant who have suffered marital breakdown.' Archbishop Worlock was making two tactical mistakes: first in advancing an opinion that was certain to be rejected, and secondly in appealing to his 'constituency' as evidence in favour of it. *Familiaris Consortio* is perfectly clear in its rejection of Archbishop Worlock's proposal: 'If these people were admitted to the Eucharist, the faithful would be led into error and confusion regarding the Church's teaching about the indissolubility of marriage' (No. 84).

So no doubt our Bishops will be reminded (in the words of article 3 of the Conclusions of the Dutch Synod) that they are to be true 'teachers' of the faith, and that they are not mere 'spokesmen' for what the laity may chance to believe. 'Neither bishops nor priests,' this text goes on, 'are the *delegates* of the faithful.' It is difficult to think of any theologian, in Holland or elsewhere, who said they were 'delegates'. But does this principle rule out all listening to and consulting of the laity? Apparently it does.

The key question is whether John Paul's perception of us is the same as our perception of ourselves. *The Easter People* has a section headed 'National Characteristics and Church

Life' (Nos. 42–6) which perfectly illustrates the problem faced by John Paul as he sits down to draft his homilies and addresses for England and Wales. Is he going to take us at our own evaluation as 'pragmatic and practical rather than speculative and theoretical', with a 'traditional respect for law', a sense of fair play and an acceptance of diversity as an enrichment? The same section also (rightly in my judgement) sees the Church in England and Wales as 'moderate' or 'middle of the road' and says that, precisely for that reason, it has escaped the extreme degree of polarization found elsewhere.

The entire visit depends on whether John Paul accepts this self-evaluation or prefers his own. Then, of course, all these supposed virtues could be stood on their heads: pragmatism would prove that we are thoroughly unprincipled, acceptance of diversity would indicate a lack of intellectual grip, and 'moderation' would make us like the shilly-shallying man of the Apocalypse who, being neither hot nor cold, is spewed out. I do not know how John Paul will tackle this question. Will the diplomatic tact of the first-time guest outweigh prophetic bluntness? Not knowing the answer will make this visit a fascinating and dramatic cliff-hanger. Its full meaning will not be unfolded until John Paul has delivered his farewell message and gone home.

Index

Index